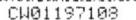

1,000,000 Books

are available to read at

Forgotten Books

www.ForgottenBooks.com

Read online
Download PDF
Purchase in print

ISBN 978-0-259-28545-8
PIBN 10166030

This book is a reproduction of an important historical work. Forgotten Books uses state-of-the-art technology to digitally reconstruct the work, preserving the original format whilst repairing imperfections present in the aged copy. In rare cases, an imperfection in the original, such as a blemish or missing page, may be replicated in our edition. We do, however, repair the vast majority of imperfections successfully; any imperfections that remain are intentionally left to preserve the state of such historical works.

Forgotten Books is a registered trademark of FB &c Ltd.
Copyright © 2018 FB &c Ltd.
FB &c Ltd, Dalton House, 60 Windsor Avenue, London, SW19 2RR.
Company number 08720141. Registered in England and Wales.

For support please visit www.forgottenbooks.com

1 MONTH OF FREE READING

at

www.ForgottenBooks.com

By purchasing this book you are eligible for one month membership to ForgottenBooks.com, giving you unlimited access to our entire collection of over 1,000,000 titles via our web site and mobile apps.

To claim your free month visit:

www.forgottenbooks.com/free166030

* Offer is valid for 45 days from date of purchase. Terms and conditions apply.

English
Français
Deutsche
Italiano
Español
Português

www.forgottenbooks.com

Mythology Photography **Fiction** Fishing Christianity **Art** Cooking Essays Buddhism Freemasonry Medicine **Biology** Music **Ancient Egypt** Evolution Carpentry Physics Dance Geology **Mathematics** Fitness Shakespeare **Folklore** Yoga Marketing **Confidence** Immortality Biographies Poetry **Psychology** Witchcraft Electronics Chemistry History **Law** Accounting **Philosophy** Anthropology Alchemy Drama Quantum Mechanics Atheism Sexual Health **Ancient History Entrepreneurship** Languages Sport Paleontology Needlework Islam **Metaphysics** Investment Archaeology Parenting Statistics Criminology **Motivational**

OF

M. DE MIRABEAU

THE ELDER,

PRONOUNCED IN THE

NATIONAL ASSEMBLY

OF FRANCE.

TO WHICH IS PREFIXED,

A SKETCH OF HIS LIFE AND CHARACTER.

I have been, I am, I will be to my grave, the man of public liberty, the man of the conſtitution. Woe to the privileged orders, if privileges conſtitute the man of the *people*, and not rather the man of the *nobles*; for *privileges* ſhall have an end, but the *people* is eternal.

MIRABEAU.

TRANSLATED FROM THE FRENCH EDITION OF M. MEJAN.

BY JAMES WHITE, ESQ.

VOLUME THE SECOND.

LONDON:
PRINTED FOR J. DEBRETT, OPPOSITE BURLINGTON-HOUSE, PICCADILLY.

M.DCC.XCII.

NEW YORK
PUBLIC
LIBRARY

CONTENTS.

                                              Page

FIRST speech of M. de Mirabeau, in support of his motion for establishing a gradual progression, in the elections to public offices — — 31

Discussion on the said motion — 54

Second speech on the same subject 60

Speech on the patriotic offer of nine hundred thousand livres, made by the republic of Geneva — — 69

Speech on the motion for expelling the Abbé Maury, who had made use of expressions offensive to the Assembly 79

Second speech on the same subject — 82

Speech on the proposition for annulling the imperative mandates, and for fixing the renewal of the Assembly, after completing the Constitution — — 90

CONTENTS.

	Page
Speech on the question, whether the king's message respecting the English armament, should be taken into immediate consideration	101
First speech on the right of making war and peace	107
Epistle dedicatory to the departments, on sending to them the said speech	197
Second speech on the same subject	205
Debate on the decree of Mirabeau	246
Additional article proposed by Mirabeau	252
Funeral eulogium on Franklin	258
Plan of an address to the French, upon the civil constitution of the clergy, adopted and presented by the ecclesiastical committee, to the National Assembly, and pronounced by M. Mirabeau	265
Speech on the measures relative to the external defence of the state	332
Presidentship of Mirabeau	355
His answer to the deputation from the quakers	357

CONTENTS.

	Page
Speeches and debates upon the regency	364
Reflections and particulars relative to the death of Mirabeau	402
Deputations and petitions relative to the same	410
Decree concerning the honours to be rendered to the memory of great men, and particularly to that of Mirabeau	422
Funeral of Mirabeau	426

ERRATUM.

In the grammatical note at the end of the speech on the right of war and peace, for *lo pueblo*, read *el pueblo*.

PREFACE.

WHEN the former part of the translated speeches of Mirabeau, was presented to the public, three remaining volumes of the original were expected from the press. I was impatient for their appearance: I felt an earnest desire to continue the task which I had undertaken: my wishes have, at length, been gratified, and this volume completes the selection of all that is most illustrious, in *The Labours of Mirabeau at the National Assembly.*

This extraordinary statesman is, I am induced to think, not universally a favourite

PREFACE.

vourite with the people of this kingdom. The servants of the government discountenance his name; the adherents of the opposition have little cause to be his admirers*. But it is for these very reasons, that I persist in being his interpreter; it is for these very reasons, that I have singled out, with avidity, his master-strokes of greatness, that I have exerted all my faculties for the extension of his renown, and endeavoured to contribute towards ensuring its immortality.

Yet, that the ministers of a monarchy should discourage the fame of men, who have been signalized as the leaders of a democratic party, is not at all astonishing; it is the duty of their place; and although, in their hearts, they may admire the

---

* See his speech on *The Address to the King, beseeching him to dismiss his ministers.* Vol. I. page 138.

works

PREFACE. iii

works of Mirabeau, they muſt accommodate their language to their ſtation. As little is to be wondered at, that the oppoſition ſhould hate a man, who ſo clearly underſtood the exact value of its patriotiſm.

In all the ungenerous pamphlets, written againſt a revolution, which, notwithſtanding its defects, ſhould not be frowned on by a free people, no exception whatever hath been made in favour of the man, who had ſtruggled to reconcile and blend the principles of democracy, with the bleſſings of a limited monarchy. The virtues and the talents of a Mirabeau are entitled, to diſtinction, and even to applauſe, from every nation which can pride herſelf in literature and liberty; and the children of ſcience and of freedom ſhould have been the laſt, to calumniate

calumniate the friend and the ornament of humanity*.

France, however, hath shewn her gratitude to the memory of him dead, who, while living, was the idol and the oracle of her legislature. If faction and self-interest waged war against his views, they scrupled not to reverence his abilities. As a politician, he occasionally experienced interruption; as an orator, he never knew what it was to be despised. The closeness of his reasoning was relieved and illustrated, by the fire and the majesty of his declamation. None coughed, none muttered curses, none stole away to dinner, when *Mirabeau* rose to speak: his admiring auditors paid him the homage of deep silence, and, when he

---

* No man was more exposed to what he himself expressively terms, " the barking of envious mediocrity."

ceased

PREFACE.

ceased, their natural deficiency of phlegm, betrayed them into the most animated proofs of approbation. No gaudy ideas, no glittering verbosity, amused the ear and the imagination at the expence of the understanding, nor distracted attention from the main subject of debate: it was not a display of fire-works, but a grand and awful discharge of artillery, doing effectual execution upon the auxiliaries of despotism.

The more completely to discredit the reputation of Mirabeau, and to inspire all Europe with an unfavourable opinion of him, a calumny, which had originated with his enemies at home, was circulated industriously through all the neighbouring kingdoms. It was reported that he was an atheist. That he was not, I most sincerely and solemnly believe. I call to witness

witness the celebrated speech, in this volume*; a speech, wherein he traces the dispensation of Christ, from the pomp which now surrounds it, to its remote and humble origin; a speech, wherein he proves, not only the triumphant excellence of that heaven-suggested system, but likewise evinces, that he understood and felt, the full importance and effect of both natural and revealed religion. Without doubt, a man of eloquence, though an unbeliever in his heart, might make a plausible and fluent discourse, upon the advantages of religion; but he could never reach the summit of that bold and fervid oratory, which, while it sends conviction into the minds of those who hear him, is an indisputable evidence of his own.

 Ministers of the holy gospel should ne-

* The speech on *The civil constitution of the Clergy.*

ver resort to calumny. Let them punish the real rebel, as they ought, and when they can; but let them not heap unjust odium on his character; lest, while asserting the Almighty's rights in one respect, they offend him most grosly in another.

To simplify, is not to destroy. Instead of branding the whole French nation, as a race of godless fools, the enraged writers of anti-revolution pamphlets, should have known that the people of France consists of three descriptions of men; of the ecclesiastic, who wishes to lead the life of a voluptuary, of the infidel, or pseudo-philosopher, and of those who, like M. Mirabeau, are friends to purified Christianity.

Deism is insufferable in a Christian land, atheism every where. I can assure my fellow-citizens, that, were there any thing in the following speeches, which, in the slightest degree, tended to vilify religion, I should be the last man living to publish it.

I am not acquainted with the private life of Mirabeau. But, it is not at all impossible, that a young nobleman, infected by fashionable society, and misled by fashionable productions, might have unwarily admitted notions, which, afterwards, reflection, and his judgment, now matured, determined him to abjure and abandon. Like the repentant publican, he might stand afar off, and, smiting his contrite breast, cry, " God be merciful to me a sinner." Like the saint, who had been the disciple of Gamaliel, he might, from having been a persecutor, become an apostle of Christianity.

Titus, the Roman emperor, and Henry
the

PREFACE. ix

the Fifth of England*, escaped from the labyrinth of error, in good time: the regenerated libertine became a luminary of devotion, and the paragon and hero of benignity.

But Titus, and Henry, and Mirabeau, had genius; genius, which lay hid under the burthen of their infirmities, and which panted for an opportunity, to vindicate the worth of its possessor.

Grattan, after his eloquent exertions on the tithe-bill, would, doubtless, have been slandered for an atheist, had there been any thing in the circumstances of his earlier life and character, which could have held out to revenge a pretence for misrepresenting him. But, as Mirabeau himself observes, there are " persons,

---

* " I will redeem the time
Upon the head of Hotspur."

" whose

"whose very name disarms calumny, and whose reputation, both as public and private men, the most headstrong libellers have never essayed to tarnish; men, in fine, who, without blemish, without views of interest, and without fear, will be honoured even to the grave, both by their friends and by their enemies *."

With respect to the late revolution, it were to be wished, that its admirers here, had learned to moderate their admiration, and forborne to pronounce public and unseasonable encomiums on it. "A foolish friend is worse than a wise enemy." An ill-timed panegyric may prove as mischievous as a satire. Hyperbolical praise provokes extravagant abuse. The

---

* See his second speech *On the Rights of War and Peace.*

art

PREFACE

art of wondering judiciously, is a useful qualification.

The new French constitution, is neither the most glorious master-piece of human wisdom, nor—a most abominable fabric of folly and impiety.

Let us cast our eyes on Europe. Government and liberty defame and defy each other. Monarchy looks around her, with suspicion, with indignation, with dismay. Aristocracy knits her brows, and seeks to hide her trepidation, under the gallant mask of fortitude. Episcopacy turns pale, and, ever and anon, raises her hand to her head, to refix her tottering mitre. Faction, meanwhile, like the god with the double face, looks two ways at once, and pleads for power and interest, in the language of patriotism.

Let us now make a grand progress, through

through thefe four divifions of the political world.

"Kings,—if once a nation be determined to become free, no artifice, no violence, on your part, can prevent her. In vain do ye befet your frontiers with troops; in vain do ye interdict what ye term feditious writings; anxiety herfelf is for a teftimony againft ye, and operates to your utter difcomfiture; fhe unclofes the fleeping eye of reafon, fhe emboldens ftrength, fhe engenders public fpirit, and re-fharpens the edge of curiofity.

Kings,—advife with the fincere, and flight the counfels of the crafty. Give ear to thofe who underftand the heart of man, who can whifper to you delicious fecrets of fubftantial popularity.

O thou, who, in the chambers of the Efcurial, art lamenting the fate of royalty,
why

why wilt thou not voluntarily and magnanimously bestow, what, otherwise, will ere long be extorted from thee? Why wilt thou not consecrate thy name to immortality; why wilt thou not become a very god amidst thy people?—Do not wait for the voice of solicitation; still less run the risk of indignity. Take pattern from your brother of Poland; gather together your wise men; frame a free constitution; then assemble the *Cortes*, and tell your delighted citizens, that you have renounced the rod of despotism.

Yes, be beforehand with the assertors of humanity. Outstrip the designs of the philanthropist and the philosopher; make it a point of virtuous jealousy, to admit of no patriot in the nation, but yourself. Do this, and your grandeur will eclipse that of the Cæsars; do this, and you will be be enrolled amongst the benefactors of the world; do this, and your dominion will be established upon adamant.

The Imperial Austrian hath just paid the debt of nature: may his successor, as first in European dignity, sigh also to be the first in beneficence, and aspire to add, to the august catalogue of his titles, the sublime appellation of THE FATHER OF CHRISTENDOM.

Arbitress of the North, your frozen empire is not yet ripe for liberty. There, philosophy and the arts are still only in their adolescence. Your subjects are but half civilized: but they will one day be free. Let your sceptre, then, lie light upon their shoulders; be the foundress of that structure, which others are to elevate; become the herald of that freedom, which is to convey the light of science, and the

balm

PREFACE. xv

balm of prosperity, to the comfortless and rude nations that are neighbours to the Pole. All great events have their forerunners. It is yours, to sow the seeds of that happiness, which your successors are to guard in its maturity; it is yours, to see that it take root; it is yours to cherish it. Suffer your people to acquire a taste for a more mild and equal government; instruct it in the rudiments of national greatness; engrave upon the public mind the first principles of liberty, principles, which no future Russian ruler may destroy. Then, when at length, the glorious duty shall be fulfilled, when the beauteous edifice shall be completed, your name will be remembered with a pious love, as the Baptist is revered, who was the harbinger of Christianity; it will be adored through an immense portion of one hemisphere;

misphere; and, should the gratitude of men invoke you, as a being more than mortal—Heaven itself will forgive them the idolatry.

Nobles of Europe, who, at this moment, are trembling for the very existence of your order, and who imagine, that the good of mankind, and the preservation of your privileges, are one and the same affair, be admonished by the fate of those degraded Aristocrates, who are now suffering for the injustice and fastidiousness of their forefathers. You yourselves are the cause of the calamities which threaten you, and which, if they do not fall on your heads, will infallibly overwhelm your posterity. All the luxuries, all the vanities, all the arrogant distinctions, which ye perpetually devise, to mortify your fellow-citizens, and to remove them

far

far away from you, serve only to provoke their envy, and to give birth to those inconvenient and alarming interrogatories, concerning the equality and original rights of men. Ye tantalize your inferiors, ye disgust them with your follies, ye afflict them with your scorn, and ye exasperate them by your iniquity. Ye live, as if ye thought, that the only real use of riches, was to expend them in the humiliation of the democracy.

Nobles of Europe, be moderate, be just; it is the only mean left for the salvation of your dignity. The ostentation of the first Cæsar proved his ruin; the more politic Augustus walked humbly before the people, and thus blunted the edge of its indignation.

Ye seem to have forgotten the very essence of your order; to have apostatized

from the genius of your inftitution. That effence, that genius, was parental, not tyrannical; it implied refpectability, not worthleffnefs; it fignified virtue, not vice; it meant wifdom, not frivolity. Would ye know what are your true privileges, what your true characteriftics, and what your proper weight in the balance of fociety, I will picture them to you, in the words of the noble Arab, who faid: " When I went out to the gate, through " the city, when I prepared my feat in " the ftreet, the young men faw me, and " hid themfelves, and the aged arofe, " and ftood up: the princes refrained from " talking, and laid their hand upon " their mouth. The nobles held their " peace, and their tongue cleaved to the " roof of their mouth. When the ear " heard me, then it bleffed me; and
" when

"when the eye saw me, it gave witness
"to me; because I delivered the poor
"that cried, and the fatherless, and him
"that had none to help him. The bles-
"sing of him that was ready to pe-
"rish, came upon me; and I caused the
"widow's heart to sing for joy. I put
"on righteousness, and it clothed me; my
"judgment was as a robe and a diadem.
"I was eyes to the blind, and feet was I
"to the lame. I was a father to the
"poor; and the cause which I knew not, I
"searched out. And I brake the jaws of the
"wicked, and plucked the spoil out of his
"teeth. My root was spread by the waters,
"and the dew lay all night upon my
"branch. My glory was fresh in me, and
"my bow was renewed in my hand. Unto
"me men gave ear, and waited, and kept
"silence at my counsel. After my words,
"they spake not again, and my speech
"dropped

"dropped upon them. And they waited
"for me, as for the rain, and they open-
"ed their mouth wide as for the latter
"rain. I chofe out their way, and fate chief,
"and dwelt as a king in the army, as one
"that comforteth the mourners."

Here, nobles of Europe, was arifto-cracy in the fublime. The Arabian Sheik, or Emir, reprefented in that ancient and divine romance, from which thefe verfes are felected, hath, in defcribing his own perfonal character and confequence, exhibited an illuftrious and precious pattern of nobility.

Difprivileged lords of France, ye cannot fay, that deftruction came upon ye unexpectedly. A rumbling found gave notice, that the earthquake was at hand.

Nobles of a certain ifland renowned for arts and arms, if you be jealous of your privileges (and well you may, for they

are

are the faireft privileges that ever peers could boaft of), evince to your fellow-citizens that you are worthy of them. Take delight in being confidered as THE FATHERS OF THE PEOPLE. Endeavour to monopolize the pre-eminence in probity. Recollect that true nobility confifts in fomething more, than in being " ftuck o'er with titles, and hung round with ftrings." Nothing, but a national conviction that you are of ufe, can fave you from the uncivil hand of contemptuous democracy. Let not the appellation of *lord* become a term of fly reproach, and the fubject of the people's raillery. Affert the native dignity of your order. Shine out in all the luftre of your anceftors. Depend, for the honour and ftability of your clafs, upon its own intrinfic excellence: for that is the grand bulwark

bulwark which you muſt raiſe for your defence, and, without that bulwark, you will prove acceſſory to your own ruin; the ariſtocracy of that iſland will become a ſelf-deſtroyer.

Abhor inſignificance, as you would a treacherous enemy, who is ſecretly undermining the foundations of your power. Repulſe the frivolity of the times; aſſemble, and take an oath, that henceforward you will do nothing that is not magnanimous and dignified; by a glorious frank-pledge become ſureties for the grandeur and renown of one another. In your prime be auguſt, when you are old, be venerable. Perſonal reſpect is the firmeſt pillar of authority; a pillar, which will outlaſt the moſt long-lived form of government, and will continue unſhakeable, amidſt all the ſhocks of of innovation. So shall the tiara remain steady upon your brows, so shall your ermined robes be kissed with filial reverence; the one shall be as a garland, bestowed as the prize of virtue, and as the symbol of bright wisdom irradiating the legislature; the other shall be to you, as the sacred mantle of Elijah, which enabled the wearer to work miracles of beneficence.

Prelates of a certain island renowned for arts and arms, I would not be understood to cast rebuke upon the men, who at present wear the mitre in that island. Few churches, in modern history, have been governed by a conclave, which, on the whole, better deserved the approbation of society. But there are privileges to be abolished, there are grievances to be redressed, which are a scandal to the people,

people, a reproach to legiflation, a ftumbling-block to government, and an outrage to Chriftianity. Is it politic, is it juft, is it humane, is it religious, that one minifter of the gofpel fhould riot in a revenue of eighteen thoufand pounds a year, and that another, perhaps alike devout, and full as learned, fhall with difficulty exift upon eighteen pounds a year? that one minifter of God's word, fhall wear purple and fine linen, and fare fumptuoufly every day, while hundreds of his fellow-minifters have not raiment for their families, have not food? To murmur at fuch a grievance, is neither fedition nor impiety, neither anarchy nor atheifm; it is the daring difcontent of reafon, and the imperative dictate of national neceffity.

Is it decent, that an ecclefiaftic, appointed

PREFACE. xxv

pointed to a bishopric, in a mountainous and rude province, remote from the metropolis, should neither understand his flock, nor be understood by them? Is it decent, or rather is it not ridiculous and profane, that a pontiff should never commune with his spiritual children, except through the medium of an interpreter? These, alas! are not the days, when the Holy Ghost would descend from heaven, in order to confer the gift of tongues. I myself have been a witness to the indecency which I censure. A confirmation was to be held in a little town amongst the hills. Several hundreds of the youth of both sexes were assembled; and, previously to the ceremony, the meek minister of the parish, was obliged to teach the prelate to pronounce by rote, what

was

was to be muttered over the heads of the juvenile congregation. Now, this is another grievance, and partakes, I vow to the Heavens, of both anarchy and impiety.

But these remote bishopricks, of moderate revenue, are too convenient to royal power, for the nation to expect, that the remedy of the abuse is to issue from that quarter. They are the first step in the ladder of episcopal promotion, a probationary state, in which the mitred candidate gives proofs of his devotion to the *ministry*. Better things are in view. The first step of the ladder is of brass, the second of silver, the third of gold and precious stones.

It is ardently to be wished, that politics would permit the prelates of that island to reside at their respective dioceses, instead of furnishing them with an excuse for lingering, during three-fourths of the year, in the midst of a luxurious capital, where they must continue passive witnesses of that spirit of dissipation, which inspires the greater part of the inhabitants. Is it absolutely requisite, that a bishop should be a baron of parliament? Can human wisdom devise no method less objectionable, of superintending the interests of religion in the legislature? Is it necessary that the clergy should be doubly represented? Is not the clergy already represented in the lower house? Do not beneficed ecclesiastics vote as freeholders, at the elections? When religion hath aught to ask from, or to suggest to, the great council, might not the pontiff communicate his sentiments to his flock,

might

might not his flock convey their joint opinion to the reprefentatives?

Again: a deep and difaftrous wound is inflicted upon Chriftianity, by your culpable want of care in the article of ordination. Hence thofe fwarms of fafhionable and unfit ecclefiaftics, who, at the prefent day, bear the opprobrious title of *buck parfons*. Should a fatal decay of difcipline take place amongft the foldiery, might not the blame, with much juftice, be imputed to the general officers? When a young man is deftined for the political adminiftration, with what anxiety, with what exercife, with what laborious ftudy, is he not educated for a poft of fo great national importance? But when a young gentleman is defigned for the facred and more momentous employment of God's miniftry, he hath little elfe to do,

PREFACE. xxix

do, with refpect to qualification, than to cut off his queüe, and change his green coat for a black one. Prelates, are ye well aware of the mifchief refulting from this carelessness? If once the laity look with contempt upon the minifters of religion, that contempt will imperceptibly extend to religion herfelf. The mafs of mankind is, in general, but too prone, to confound the function with the functionary. He who is to inftruct others, fhould have more wifdom than his audience, he who is to be their model fhould have more piety *.

* Many, however, of our young clergymen (I myfelf am acquainted with many) are an honour to their profeffion.—But no thanks to the bifhops for that. Here too let us not forget the praife which is fo defervedly beftowed, by all travellers into Scotland, upon the clergy of that kingdom.

A fenfible

Here, then, ye men of God, are still other privileges, which call for abolition, and to murmur at which, is neither anarchy nor atheism.

A sensible and worthy traveller *, of the present day, relates, that, in Spain, the meeting of two prelates is a phænomenon. There, the moment that a churchman accepts the honours of episcopacy, he takes leave of the court, and of the great world, for ever, and, retiring to his diocese, surrenders up his time to the edification of those, whom Heaven hath entrusted to his vigilance and piety. Once in his life, and but once, should a bishop be seen at levee; his name should never re-echo through the precincts of the palace, but on the day when

* The Rev. Joseph Townsend.

he

he comes to thank his royal patron for his mitre.

But your residence in the capital, and your attendance at court, are venial, in comparison of the inhuman inequality, between your splendid incomes and the deplorable estates, assigned to too many of the subaltern clergy. The fault, it must be admitted, is not altogether yours: you leave things as you found them: nevertheless, it is a trespass, in the opinion of a great people, that you are employing no measures for the mitigation of this calamity. Notwithstanding queen Ann's bounty, and the compassionate donations occasionally bestowed, very many of the most assiduous of the labourers in Christ's vineyard, have nothing like a sufficient livelihood. Their condition is a stigma on a state professing Christianity.

Every

Every minister of the gospel should have one hundred pounds a year; every married minister of the gospel, at least, one hundred and fifty. Away with pluralities, with non-residence, with sinecures. Will no voice rouse the legislature to debate upon these grievances? Should it ever be my lot, to become a member of that assembly, I will agitate these questions, if not with ability, at least with zeal. I will alarm the pontiffs and great men of the land; I will cry, woe to the *privileged orders* of ecclesiastics, and woe to that whole government, who supinely survey the misery of God's ministers. I will; unless some able and honest senator, some man of the *true* party, shall anticipate my design, and gloriously defraud me of a glorious popularity.

But, to descend from these aerial heights,

to the level of that discreet phlegm, so acceptable, so dear, to the heart of many an English *man*, and to continue the circuit of my proposed animadversions:

Men of faction, were ye but aware, of the disadvantages which attend on your unwise career of politics, we should not every day behold so many men of undoubted talents, depreciating their own worth, and disappointing their own hopes. The mind of the factious man becomes the victim of infatuation. Faction narrows the heart, faction blinds the understanding. Party, on the contrary, enlightens the understanding, and enlarges the heart. True party hath a tendency to elevate the soul, and to refine the intellectual faculties. Therefore, whenever ye see a person of abilities, entangled in selfish, cunning, inconsistent operations, rest assured, that faction hath entered into his heart, and that she is tormenting him, after the manner of a dæmon. The man of genius then becomes a dunce, the philosopher a fool, the man of-argument sophistical, the declaimer outrageous, the man of temper irritable, and he who never possessed temper, worse than ever he was before; the warrior stains his scarlet, the judge his ermine, and the " saint in lawn," sullies the whiteness of his sleeves.

It hath been concisely said by Montesquieu, that *the constitution of England is a democracy, under the mask of monarchy.* Were that philosopher now alive, we might supply him with another pithy sentence; namely, *that the legislative body of Britain, is an aristocracy under the mask of democracy.* I apprehend, that this notion is not a new one, though, perhaps, it may not have been pronounced exactly in the present form.

The fiefless nobles of Britain possess no *avowed* privileges, which are not useful and necessary to her system of social order. It is the *secret* privilege of extending their influence, through every pore and fibre of the body politic, which it behoves the British people to oppose, and to abolish. The influence of the aristocracy is a subtile and penetrating acid, which hath soaked into the entire mass of the constitution.

I have just repeated an idea, which I observed was not a new one: I will now advance another, which I believe is not a trite one. No person, who, in any part of the British empire, is a member of the aristocracy,

aristocracy, can, consistently with principles, be permitted to act as a representative of the democracy. This is more than absurd; it is a very great abuse. Indeed, with respect to too many things in this world, we live in a perpetual delusion. This aukward, unconstitutional, and dangerous circumstance, is suffered to remain uncensured. It is *aukward*, that a person who professes democracy, should be decorated with the trappings of aristocracy. The words *noble lord* should never be heard within the walls of the democratic assembly. It is *unconstitutional*, that he who, in one part of the British dominions, is by birth, by habits, and by privilege an aristocrate, should, in another, be a member of the democracy. To-day, he is a simple plebeian; next week (for he hath only to cross the Channel), he will be

a patria patrician; the week after, he may again relapse into his democratic character, and, the week after that, he may be again a gallant noble. This is pleasant conjuration. It is *dangerous*, that an hereditary member of the aristocracy, should be suffered to become a representative of the people. He cannot serve God and Mammon. For, either he will carry with him into the House of Commons, the lordly spirit of nobility, and retain the towering prejudices peculiar to that order, or he will bring back with him into the House of Peers, the leaven of democracy, which may create a fermentation, where no such fermentation should exist.

To such a senator the commons might say: Depart, you wear a coronet; you are not one of us; associate with persons of your own order, with patricians. And here let me declare, that I would not be underſtood to throw any perſonal reflection, on ſuch titled individuals, as at preſent enjoy ſeats in the Britiſh Houſe of Commons; many of them are worthy noblemen; but it is becauſe they are noblemen, that I wiſh they were not there *.

Again: Suppoſe a queſtion to be brought forward in the Engliſh Houſe of Commons, which queſtion materially concerns the democratic intereſt. This commoner of the half blood, begotten by luſty

---

* When the tribunitian authority was firſt inſtituted at Rome, a law was paſſed, prohibiting any patrician from exerciſing the office of tribune. The violation of this law, in the latter days of the republic, was one great cauſe of the deſtruction of Roman liberty.

Democracy

Democracy on condescending Aristocracy, this patricio-plebeian senator, will find himself in a disgraceful dilemma. If, true to his hereditary character, he oppose the people, in the people's own house, with what face can he presume to sit there? But what if he support the question? and what if such another question should be agitated in the Irish parliament? Will the noble lord, when with breathless haste he enters the Hibernian House of Peers, become, on a sudden, infected with the contagion of aristocracy, and utter principles the very reverse of his late patriotism in the British legislature?—This, then, is one of the numerous instances, in which the subtile acid of aristocracy, is eating its way through the whole mass of the constitution. I say, the whole mass; for if the aristocracy, either openly or *covertly*, usurp an influence in the democratic assembly, it may afterwards overawe the throne, and then the entire constitution will be at the mercy of the aristocracy.

Again: a considerable portion of the lower house, is composed of the tender nurslings of aristocracy; of eldest, and of younger sons of peers; the former of whom have a certainty, the latter a chance, of being one day summoned to forsake the democracy, and to put on all the pride, and all the privileges of nobility. Yet here have we less cause to be alarmed, than at the irregularity abovementioned. These youths are, as yet, no more than public gentlemen; and there is reason to believe and hope, that, even when hereafter uplifted to aristocracy,

PREFACE. xli

cracy, they will preserve a *kind* remembrance, of their old companions, the plebeians.

The French have been dissatisfied, because they could not consolidate the commons and the nobility, into one national assembly. Whereas it behoves us, to keep the two orders far asunder; for upon the just balance of the three powers of our triple-headed constitution, depends its prosperity, depends its existence.

Such, therefore, are the privileges which ought to be abolished, and to abolish which, were neither anarchy nor atheism.

But these, and some other abuses, already murmured at in this preface, may be remedied with gravity, with legislative sobriety; means which are far preferable to the fever of revolution. But,

even

even could they no otherwise be done away, than at the expence of a revolution, let them continue where they are, and gently decay in concert with that invaluable syftem, which, like all human things, cannot exift for ever and ever.

Having thus far affumed the ftate and deportment of an author, let me fubjoin a few paragraphs, in the character of a tranflator.

A book, and particularly a French book, is not always the worfe for being interpreted into Englifh. There is a fuperior degree of vigour in the Englifh tongue, which peculiarly adapts it to works of popular eloquence. But, befides this national advantage, a fentence may be expreffed more neatly, a phrafe turned more elegantly, a period rounded off more harmoniously and more forcibly, in

the

the tranflation, than it is in the original. This obfervation, however, is to be confined to tranflations from the modern languages, and, ftill further, to profe productions. No tranflator, I am bold to fay, can do juftice to Demofthenes. Cicero, indeed, may receive lefs injury, nay, in fome refpects, may be benefited by the hand of a tranflator: his immoderately long periods may be judicioufly divided, his tedious, and fometimes unfeafonable parenthefes, refitted, and reduced to better difcipline; but no living language can fupply a proper fubftitute, for the melody of his words, and for the harmony of his compofition.

In afferting that Englifh tranflation may prove favourable to foreign writings, I fpeak not from perfonal vanity. I fpeak, becaufe I am fenfible that what I fay is

true;

true; I am contending for the copiousness, the manliness, the vigour, the sterling weight, in a word, for the air of liberty, which characterize our language. A prose production, especially of eloquence, may not only be done justice to in an English dress, but absolutely improved. And, if the colouring may be rendered more vivid, the drawing also may be rendered more correct, and the features stronger, and more prominent; the attitudes may be ennobled, and adorned with a new grace; and, here and there, a lurking beauty may be called forth into light; in fine, a harmonizing tint may be thrown over the whole, which, perhaps, it did not possess in the original *.

It

---

* But foreigners may sometimes return us the favour. I have heard it remarked, more than once, that

It is, however, the duty of a translator, to imitate, as much as possible, the sound, and not only the sound, but even the very shape of his author's words and sentences; and, by a kind of polygraphic art, to take him off in every hue and lineament.

As to poetry, in the living languages, neither we, nor other nations, can boast the same advantages of translation. The spirit evaporates, the grace is lost. The renowned knight of La Mancha, as Cervantes informs us, happened to enter a printer's work-room, where the press was occupied by a translation in verse, of the *Orlando Furioso*. The hero read a few passages of it, and then made the follow-

---

that *Locke's Essay* reads better in the French translation, than in the original. The same remark hath been made with respect to *Hume's History of England*, elegant as that work is in our native tongue.

ing ingenious, and for the moſt part, true remark; that tranſlations in verſe, from modern poetry, were like the wrong ſide of a piece of tapeſtry, where, indeed, one ſees the figures, but the ſpirit and glow of the workmanſhip have vaniſhed, and where the whole is diſgraced by the knots and thrums of the worſteds.—To this remark, I have one exception to make, and that is in favour of Fairfax's Taſſo, which, though tranſlated in the days of Cromwell, is, for ſtrength, harmony, and likeneſs to the original, highly worthy of the eſteem of all who are addicted to polite literature. This book, like many other excellent books, is become ſcarce. As to the poetry of the ancients, Dryden and Pope have done for Virgil and Homer, the beſt that Engliſh verſe enabled them to do; and

our

PREFACE.

our venerable tranſlators of the Bible, in which there is much poetry, have ſucceeded, ſo as to be entitled to the admiration of ſucceſſive ages.

Before I quit the topic of tranſlation, let me take this opportunity of ſaying a few words, with reſpect to one other book, which well deſerves the eſtimation of the public. Though it be a work of a different nature from the orations of Mirabeau, it may not appear altogether unconnected, with the grandeur and proſperity of empires. It ſhall, therefore, come in by way of epiſode.

The production alluded to, is that valuable little book of the benignant and illuſtrious archbiſhop of Cambray, the title of which may be thus engliſhed: *Inſtructions for the Education of a Daughter.* This book I had eagerly ſought for, and as eagerly

eagerly tranflated. I had never heard that it exifted in an Englifh drefs. However, when I propofed it to the bookfellers, fome anfwered, that they had never before heard of fuch a book; others, that it had been tranflated many years ago; others obferved, that it muft be now too old-fafhioned; while others again had the temerity to infer, from its being little known, that the book itfelf had never been of any value.

Neverthelefs, if we may be allowed to hazard a conjecture, the true objection was, that the nation was about to be gratified with a new publication of Madame de Sillery, who is better known by her late title of Countefs de Genlis. I think well of the labours, and pay homage to the good intentions, of this philanthropic woman of quality. But I am very apprehenfive, prehensive, that to write *effectually*, upon the great business of education, and, still more, upon the education of damsels, is a task above the strength of womankind. The writings of Madame de Genlis may, doubtless, do *some* good; but, like all other female systems of female education, they are materially and radically defective. I fear that the ladies only skim the surface of things. With respect to the education of damsels, there are certain reasons which render it impossible, for a woman to write upon it with completeness and fidelity.

I therefore strenuously call the attention of the public, to the compact, but able treatise of the archbishop of Cambray. If I am not to publish it, at least I will recommend it. Those who cultivate the French tongue, will do well to enquire

PREFACE.

for the original; the English reader will be fortunate, in procuring that old translation, if, indeed, any such exists. As for mine, which I had accompanied with notes and a preface, containing divers useful, comical, and comfortable observations, I shall, one of these days, cause two or three hundred copies of it to be printed; which copies I mean to give away, to such as may consider the present worth accepting. This will probably become productive of still further benefit; for then perhaps some person will dare to pirate the translation, and thus the public will obtain it at last [*].

And

---

[*] I cannot here refrain from relating another odd and unpleasant circumstance. As the mind must not always remain on the rack of politics, I sometimes amuse myself with writing story-books. And why not; if so grave a man as the archbishop o
Cambray

PREFACE.

And here the question may be started, why this production of the great Fenelon, should have dwindled out of fashion, while his Telemachus still triumphs over caprice and false taste. I will endeavour to answer this interrogatory.

Our great-grandmothers (for the book was written at the close of the last cen-

Cambray condescended to write fairy tales? (*Vide* the French grammar.) I had produced an original work, which I called the *New Arabian Nights Entertainments*. But behold, when I applied to a bookseller, I was informed that there was actually in the press, a translation of a French work, of the very same nature, and of which I had never till then heard. When this last shall come forth, I hope the public will be pleased with it; but I hope, likewise, that my *home manufacture*, my *English* New Arabian Tales, will not be utterly despised, in favour of the foreigner. For, verily, there are some stories in mine, to which the caliph Haroun Alraschid would e been very glad to listen.

tury) imagined that the archbishop, of Cambray saw too much of them; that he told more than was convenient to them; that he turned the heart of woman inside out; that he was labouring to make them angels, while they themselves were determined to continue human. Accordingly, the work went out of fashion. Your great-grandmothers belied to your grandmothers, both the bishop and his book; and your grandmothers defamed him to your mothers. At length, new treatises began to come *into* fashion. Gentle essays were composed by females, upon female education. The women eagerly resorted to writers of their own sex, who had a fellow-feeling for their common infirmities; to writers, who either winked at, or could not see, the fundamental mistakes and blemishes of womankind; to writers

who

PREFACE.

who confined themselves to the cultivation of the manners, while they left the heart and the understanding a prey to barrenness and desolation. In fine, the sex fled for shelter, to perfidious mildness and superficial philosophy, from him who was addressing them with the affection of a parent, and with the fervour of an apostle.

Ah! my children (for sometimes I affect to be old and inconsiderable), my children, in this, as well as in many other instances a she-friend is not always the best that you can have. You are the most beautiful women upon earth, and I wish to see you the most rational. Do justice, ah! do justice to that spirit and that capacity, with which nature, in a transport of partiality, hath endowed you. Recollect, my fair fellow-citizens, that
the

the fate of empire depends on *you*; that the juſt influence, which it becomes you to poſſeſs in civil ſociety, is the teſt and the guardian of our virtue: for, whereſoever the women begin to be held in diſeſteem, it is an indubitable ſign, that they have ſuffered frivolity and profligacy to uſurp the throne of ſenſe and honour, and that nation is declining to its downfall.

There is one point, in particular, to which I entreat you to pay immediate attention. Women are naturally proud; but fine women are ſtill prouder than women who are not fine; but a fine woman of *quality*, is the proudeſt of all fine beings. Take care, my children (I mean you who enjoy rank and titles); theſe are not the days, when it is a ſafe thing to be haughty. There is a powerful and untameable

tameable spirit gone abroad, and it were prudence not to provoke it. The petty piques of women have produced wonderful vicissitudes, in matters of far greater moment. In ancient Rome, the petty pique of a plebeian lady, gave occasion to that grand victory, by which the people obtained a share in the consulship. It was objected to the late duchesses and countesses of France, that, while they hurried through the streets of Paris in their carriages, they looked down upon the rest of mankind, as it were upon the very outcasts of society*. The plain wife of the plebeian treasures up the remembrance of the scornful aspect, with which her insolent superior had surveyed her. "*That woman*" discloses her chagrin to her husband, and "*that man*" re-com-

---

* Mercier's *Tableau de Paris*.

municates it to his neighbours; the contagion spreads, and the odium and the enemies of aristocracy are augmented. Take care, my children; for these are not the days when it is a safe thing to be haughty. Does an affable and humane deportment diminish the lustre of your beauty, or the antiquity of your pedigree, or the number of your footmen, and lovers?—But this is wandering too far; this belongs with more propriety, to the preface of the little book of the archbishop of Cambray.

Heed not fashion, then, my children, in the important concern of education, but return with filial reverence, to those who offer you instruction, which is both solid and efficacious; nor rest all your hopes upon the *light summer morality*, which

which flows from the ruby lips of the ladies.

But to be grave—It hath been well obferved, that if ever there were an angel in human shape, it was Fenelon. A man of genius, without affecting eccentricity, a man of learning without being arrogant, a courtier of Louis XIV. yet the indefatigable foe of despotism*, he remarked, at once with penetration and with regret, the political and moral wretchedness of the kingdom which gave him being, and dedicated his life and talents to her service. The amiableness of his manners shed a lustre upon his wisdom, and reconciled

---

* When that monarch first read Telemachus, he is said to have exclaimed; "Here is a man who tells me, that I have been, for these fifty years, mistaking the art of reigning."—He could never after endure Fenelon. He used to call him *a writer of po- -al romances.*

the heart to his correction. With that eloquence in which Locke was deficient, and uninfected by that vanity*, for which Rouſſeau is contemptible, he reaſons without dryneſs, and invites attention without paradox. His Telemachus and *L'Education des Filles* are immortal proofs of my aſſertion, and ineſtimable monuments of his anxiety for thoſe, who moſt require the care of the prieſt and the philoſopher. Yes, the education of youth was the prime object of his labours; for this he meditated, for this he amaſſed the treaſures of antiquity, for this he explored the ſcriptures; but while delivering the reſult of his reflections and reſearches, with that purity and

* The moſt miſerable of all vanities, that of affecting to think differently from the bulk of mankind, with reſpect to the great points of Chriſtian revelation.

ſweetneſs

PREFACE. lix

sweetness so distinguishable in his style, no insinuation ever escaped him, which might tend to offer insult, to the undeniable and incomparable truths of Christianity.

Nor were his virtues, as a politician, less precious. Profound, enlightened, liberal, he saw, he felt, what was due to the dignity and prosperity of man, and, as far as he could discreetly, in a nation whose chief was absolute, confessed himself the advocate of liberty *. Here

---

* It was universally believed, that had his royal pupil lived to wear the crown of France, the generous youth would have restored the liberties of the people.—In mentioning Fenelon as a politician, we ought not to forget his *Proper Heads for the Self-examination of a King* (another book out of fashion), in which the famous subject of *the Balance of Power*, is handled with ability, and, what is better, with tue.

again that delightful and almoſt divine book, which he compoſed for the inſtruction of the young duke of Burgundy, preſents itſelf as a proof of his philanthropy. "If," ſays the Abbé Terraſſon, "the happineſs of the human race can "be the effect of an epic poem, the Te- "lemachus is the nobleſt preſent the "Muſes ever made to mankind."

Books, which flatter the weakneſſes of nature and of the times, will, in general, meet with a more ſudden and more warm reception, than ſincere and ſolid writings, which tell us what we are, and what we ſhould be. But, when this faſhionable rage is ſpent, and ſpent at laſt it will be, common ſenſe begins to pry into the dungeons of obſcurity, for deſert which lies neglected and forgotten. The deſpiſed volume is at length elevated to a juſt and
laſting

PREFACE.

lasting fame, while the minion of frail fashion is committed to irretrievable oblivion. Until the reign of queen Anne, the *Paradise Lost* of Milton was little noticed, was little known; it did not suit the public taste. At length Addison took fire at his undeserved fate, and re-ushered it into the presence of his countrymen. Such also, for a time, was the fate of our adored Shakespeare. There is some merit, and I swear there is much pleasure, in rescuing from disgrace, a production which deserves to be eternal.

Perhaps, with regard to Fenelon, I may seem to fall into that indiscreet admiration, to which I myself have made objections in a former paragraph. But, I am not commending the bishop's little book, merely as a good piece of writing; object and intent of the author are

what

what I applaud; it is their producible effect, which I admire in idea, and which hath led me to this high praise, which just saves me soaring into hyperbole.

There is often, in men of parts, a cruel deficiency of judgment; cruel, since it is the cause of their doing harm to humankind. Eloquence, and what is usually termed wit, and even the sublimer powers of the imagination, in a word, *genius* may exist in men, unaccompanied by that sort of ability, called *judgment*. The former is, perhaps, the result of particular temperament, and of a happy configuration of the intellectual apparatus. Might not the latter be thus defined: the grace of God, directing a wise and good man, to what is best for himself and for society?

May we ever have such men, for ou

senator

senators, for our magistrates, for our ministers. Grant us, ye Heavens, but this, and all will yet be well. For there is, in Britons, a kind of native, constitutional good sense, an inveterate solidity, that will, in spite of all the efforts of folly to degrade them, bear them up to the very last, and snatch their manners from degeneracy *.

* Having now finished the pleasing task of interpreting the eloquence of *Mirabeau*, it is my intention to proceed immediately to translate the well-written History of the Revolution of France, by M. *Rabaut de Saint-Etienne*. This latter work will operate as a kind of commentary on the former.——In the following pages, I have deviated somewhat from the usual mode of pointing, and endeavoured to imitate that of the ancients, which referred less to the sense, than to the harmony of the composition.

SPEECHES

OF

M. DE MIRABEAU.

Letter written by M. De Caraman *to M.* De Mirabeau [*].

March 20, 1789.

I HERE inclose, my lord, the two very affecting letters, which you have been so good to entrust to my perusal; they have impressed me with the deepest anxiety

[*] This letter, and the answer to it, together with the three subsequent articles, would have appeared with more propriety, in the first volume of the trans-lated

iety for one of the moſt reſpectable of men*, and for whom I have the greateſt affection. God grant that the firſt news we hear, may be to inform us of his recovery. The flattering reception which you met with at Marſeilles, hath, doubtleſs, given you ſtrong aſſurances of the confidence repoſed in you, by the inhabitants of that great city; and you are too much in love with order, which alone can enſure ſucceſs to the preſent object of the miniſtry, not to be ſenſible of the conſe-

lated ſpeeches of M. *de Mirabeau*. But my original intention was, to give only a few ſpecimens of his oratorical abilities, and not a complete ſelection of whatever could be moſt intereſting to an Engliſh reader, in the works of that great man. Is it not better that the articles above mentioned ſhould be introduced even thus aukwardly, than not at all?

* The father of M. Mirabeau.

quences of numerous assemblies, at a juncture when there reigns, I cannot tell for what reason, an afflicting effervescence. You understand me sufficiently, to dispense with my saying any thing more to you upon this subject. A mark of friendship and gratitude ought not to alarm the public; but you cannot give a greater proof of your love for the king, and for the happiness of the kingdom, than by calming those unquiet spirits, whom it became to look forward to the assembly of the States-General, as the only principle of national prosperity. It is by a calm line of conduct, that their confidence and friendship should be shewn to you; and I expect it from yours. It is the prime object of the king's wishes, and if there be a moment, when such conduct should become a *principle*, it is when the nation is assembling under the inspection of its monarch, in order to prepare a regeneration, capable of ensuring to it a lasting felicity.

I have the honour to be, with sincere attachment,

    My Lord,

        Your most humble

            And most obedient servant,

                The Count de CARAMAN.

M. MIRABEAU's *Answer*.

TWO things, my lord, equally astonish me in your letter; the interpretation which you put upon the word *public*, and the doubts which you express with regard to the true reason, of what you are pleased to term an afflicting effervescence.

For

For the univerfal difcontent, which you confider as an effervefcence, there are certain reafons, or motives, too notorious, not to do away every doubt which you entertain.

And firft; the people is perifhing of hunger—There is one reafon.—The chief perfons entrufted with authority in this province*, are accufed of having, for thefe forty years, robbed the public of its corn.—There is another reafon for you.

The infolence and injuftice of the privileged orders are increafing every day: and there is a third reafon.

It is matter of indignation, that, in contempt of the known intentions of the king, of the clear letter of his laws, &c. the benefit which he defigns for the na-

* Provence.

tion should be counteracted: or rather, that, with all the rage of pride and ambition combined, endeavours should be made to render it impossible.—There is a fourth reason.

It is a real subject of alarm, to see that the king's commissioners, men most intimately connected with persons in office, have entirely fallen off from their party.— There, my lord, you have a fifth reason.

We are grieved to the very heart, that the parliament should persist in trying and hanging wretches, whom famine alone had tempted to transgress the bounds of law; that the bishop of Sisteron should scatter pardon with a loud voice, and vengeance in a soft one; that you should yield, in contradiction to your principles and your natural benevolence, to treacherous and unjust applications to send troops,

troops, to a place where troops have nothing at all to do, and where there is likely to be no disturbance, but what our enemies wish to make; troops who may bring a deluge of mischiefs upon the province, and who will never be of any use, excepting to the pride and vengeance of their worships of the long robe.—There now is a large assortment of other reasons for discontent, and I suppress a thousand more, from a regard for your sensibility.

And now I make bold to ask you, of whom consists that public, *whom the marks of love and gratitude which I receive, so much alarm?*——Men in office, when will you learn, that your clubs, and your levee-hunters, and your sycophants, are not the public?—Figure to yourself, my lord, a hundred and twenty thousand individuals

dividuals at Marseilles, a whole city, so
industrious and so commercial, incurring
the loss of a day's labour, the windows
hired out at one or two louis each, and
horses at the same rate; the coach of that
man whose only merit was his love of
equity, covered over with palm-branches,
boughs of laurel and of olive; the people
kissing the wheels; the women presenting
to him their infants as an offering; a hundred and twenty thousand voices, from the
mousse to the *millionaire* *, rending the heavens with acclamations, and shouting *Vive
le roi* and * * * *; four or five hundred
youths of the first families in the city, pre-
ceding him on horseback; three hundred
coaches following him; imagine this, my

* From the poorest of the rabble to the merchant
worth a plum.

lord,

lord, and you will have a just idea of my departure from Marseilles. You will also discover, first, that the *possedans-fiefs** of Aix are not the public; 2dly, that it is as impossible to prevent such an *effervescence*, (since you are pleased to give it that term) as it is, my lord, to provoke it; 3dly, that men are more apt to run into the submissiveness of gratitude, than into the excesses of licentiousness; 4thly, in fine, that there was no other method of escaping all those honours, than to flee from a post, to desert which were both cowardice and ingratitude.—And now, do you think that such an honourable, but embarrassing escort, was conducted in so bad a manner, as to give you reason to complain of it? And, if you do not complain of it, why

* Persons possessing fiefs.

do

do you deliver up your friends to your enemies, thofe who applaud you to thofe who hifs you?

I have the honour to be, with great refpect,

    My Lord,

        Your moft humble

            And moft obedient fervant,

                The Count de MIRABEAU.

THE FRENCH EDITOR

TO

THE READER.

THE name of M. MIRABEAU is so connected with all the successes of the National Assembly, that, in publishing a collection of the labours of that philosophic legislator, we seem to be also publishing *almost* a history of the assembly itself.

You will not, then, take it amiss, that these articles are here inserted, which were written by M. de Mirabeau himself, at the æra of the opening of the States-General; they naturally form a preface to this work, since they contain a history of what was

was *thought*, on the eve, and on the birthday of that assembly, whose memorable acts, particularly the first, will obtain the blessings of the French, and the admiration of the world.

The genuine merit of these three articles is moreover evinced, by those wretched orders of council, which forbade their publication, to the great scandal of justice and of common sense.

But *justice, common sense, and ministers of state* were then what they had ever been; three things perfectly distinct, and so very hostile to one another, that time, which reconciles all things, could but seldom exhibit to us the consoling spectacle of their union.

Account of what paſſed at Verſailles, on the 2d of May, 1789.

" BEFORE we ſpeak of the ceremony which preceded the opening of the States-General, we think we ought to devote a few lines to the preſentation, which took place on Saturday the 2d of May. Not that we deſign to enlarge upon affairs of mere etiquette; there are publications enough, which give a very accurate account of thoſe unimportant objects, and we do not imagine that details of that kind, are what the public expects from us.

" We ſhall confine ourſelves, then, to mentioning, that, after being ſucceſſively aſſembled in the hall of Hercules, the deputies of the three orders were admitted to the king; thoſe of the clergy and the nobility

bility were admitted into the king's closet, those of the commons into the hall of Louis XIV.

"Nothing remarkable passed there; we were struck, however, with the little solemnity observed in a presentation, which ought certainly to have been dignified, with the want of regularity, with the difficulties, the delays, occasioned by an inaccurate list of the bailiwicks and seneschalties. We shall not notice the distinction of customs universally disapproved, and too important in their political consequences, not to be treated of separately, when the National Assembly shall take cognizance of such matters.

"One singularity there was, which gave rise to observations equally unfavourable; and that was, the difference in the mode

mode of prefenting the three orders*. The commons felt themfelves hurt: feveral groupes were immediately formed. It was propofed with fome degree of vehemence, to carry, that very inftant, a remonftrance to the foot of the throne, and to reprefent to the king how afflicting were fuch diftinctions, to that portion of the three orders which was truly national.

" The opinion which prevailed was as follows: —The firft fenfation which the appearance of the commons fhall excite in the king's breaft, ought not to be a painful one; and fuch muft be the fenfation occafioned to a good prince, by the fear either of difobliging, or of having difobliged. Befides, the prefentation is

* They were received in different apartments. Add to this, that both the folding-doors were thrown open for the clergy, and only one for the nobility.

purely

purely optional, and not at all obligatory or legal. The king in his own houfe, receives whom he pleafes, and how he pleafes. The code of etiquette hath been hitherto the facred fire, adored by men of the court and of the privileged orders; it does not become the nation to afcribe to it the fame importance. It is, when fhe fhall demand the abolition of all humiliating diftinctions; and that the teftimonies of refpect allotted to the monarch, and which cannot be too great, fince a people honours itfelf, in paying honours to its prince, may be uniform and univerfal; becaufe variations in that point are no longer a tribute of honour, but a fymbol of flavery; then it is, that we may quote this recent inftance of fervile ceremonioufnefs. At prefent, we are only fo many individuals, to whom the provifional

fional legiflator hath not yet opened his lips. What, gentlemen! when it fhall be lawful for us to fpeak, fhall we not have objects of more confequence to occupy our attention, than the names of the halls and ftair-cafes, through which we have been conducted by the Mafter of the Ceremonies?

" And now let us relate an incident of another kind, and which we confider as a real victory obtained for the popular caufe.

" An irregular deputation, nominated in Provence by that part of the nobility who are willing neither to contribute to the public expences, nor to admit of a reformation in the ftates of that province, had been put upon the lift of the Grand Mafter of the Ceremonies, in order to have the honour of being prefented to the king, as conftituting the deputation from the nobility of Provence. The king refufed to receive it; and admitted the legal deputation only, which had been appointed by the fenefchalties *.

" This event is worthy of notice, as it in fome meafure determined beforehand the exclufion of thefe pretended deputies, who might have obftinately traverfed the operations of the people; for *the Poffedans-fiefs* went fo far as to enter a previous

---

* The deputies of Provence, who arrived at Verfailles on the firft of May, apprehenfive that the eight pretended deputies of *the Poffedans-fiefs* might, by their intrigues, obtain permiffion to be prefented to the king as deputies, addreffed a letter to him in terms of great refpect, but great energy, for the purpofe of preventing the prefentation of the pfeudo-deputies.

protest against whatever might be done by the assembly of the states-general *."

Account of what passed at Versailles on May 4th, 1789.

" THE ceremony of the procession of the deputies was conducted with very great solemnity. The deputies of the three orders, or rather the representatives of the nation, attended the king at the church of Notre-Dame de Versailles, where that Prince was received with acclamations, which, doubtless, are an earnest of the

* After this paragraph, in the original, follows a long account of the disputes in Provence, between the nobles possessing fiefs, and the *fiefless* nobility, the latter being refused admittance into the provincial assembly, by the former. I omit this account, as uninteresting to English readers. W.

recompence which is due to what he is doing for the welfare of his people.

" From Notre-Dame they all repaired to the church of St. Louis, the commons in a body, the nobility and the clergy following them, and the king and the royal family bringing up the rear.

" Here all the pomp of royalty, and of the court, was displayed.

" Divine service was performed. After the gospel, the bishop of Nancy ascended the pulpit. *Religion is the strength of kingdoms; religion is the sole and never-failing source of their prosperity:* such was the division of his discourse.

" It was prolix, and appeared to consist of shreds tacked together, without ideas, without style, without effect. It was quite another sort of eloquence, quite another sort of inspiration, in a word, quite another order of things, that we had expected

pected in this august assembly. Every common-place topic, from the baptism of Clovis to the illness of Louis the Well-beloved * at Metz, and from declamations against luxury down to railing against philosophy, found room in this extraordinary sermon. It was but too plain, that the orator was not perfectly satisfied with himself, that he had neither plan nor fixt object, and that he entirely mistook the juncture.

" There was one passage which met with considerable applause. The point related to the operations of the treasury, to the wretchedness experienced by the country parts of the kingdom, to the condition of the peasantry. The orator concluded a rhetorical amplification with these words: *And it is in the name of a good king, of a monarch just and tender-hearted, that those abominable extortioners practise*

* The late king.

such barbarities. The church refounded with the approbation of the commons."

" Another ftroke is worthy of obfervation. FRANCE, THY WILL IS SUFFICIENT! The whole fermon fhould have been an explanation of that happy text.

" The frequent panegyrics on the king were much commended; but they might have been brought in better, and delivered with more felicity of expreffion.

" The apoftrophe to the queen, *Daughter of the Cæfars, rival and confidante of the beneficence of her auguft fpoufe!* might have been more oratorical, and lefs awkwardly introduced.

" This difcourfe, like our modern tragedies, was entirely compofed of hemifticks: never was there a finer opportunity for a difplay of eloquence, and never was fuch an opportunity fo completely neglected."

Account

Account of what paſſed at Verſailles on the 5th of May, 1789.

" AT length, on this day, the opening of the ſtates-general took place.

" Notice had been given to the deputies to repair to the hall at eight o'clock. They waited a long time, in a dark and narrow corridor, before the buſineſs of calling over the names was begun; and, really, they looked more like a crowd of merchants upon 'Change, than deputies in the veſtibule of the National Aſſembly.

" In calling over the names, the order of the bailiwicks in 1614 was followed. It were difficult to put the patience of the deputies to a more indiſcreet and fatiguing trial; and one might readily be tempted to imagine, that it required ſome ingenuity to devife a form fo capricious, fo complicated, fo difgufting.

"The coup d'œil of the hall was fuperb. The deputies were not feated until a quarter before twelve, and the king made his appearance almoft immediately after. He was received with loud applaufe. The queen placed herfelf befide him, but not under the canopy, on a feat fomewhat lower than the throne; the royal family and the king's attendants furrounded them.

"The king read a difcourfe, in which he expreffed much purity of fentiment, and manifefted paternal intentions. He was feveral times interrupted by acclamations; and this fort of interruption appeared excufable, and even ornamental, on account of its fincerity.

"The keeper of the feals fpoke for a
confiderable

confiderable time; but three fourths of the affembly did not hear one word he faid.

"The director-general of the finances then read a volume, which was far from being a fmall one. The king, in finifhing his difcourfe, had declared, that this minifter fhould lay before us an account of the condition of the finances; and thus were we deprived of the pretence, and even of the means of difputing the word of the director-general, who was not entitled to fpeak in the ftates-general, without fpecial permiffion, fince the chancellor, or the officer fupplying his place, is the only commiffioner of the king who fits in that affembly. M. Necker fpoke for three hours, and more.

"It were imprudent to attempt giving an account of a fpeech of fuch great length,

length, without having it before one's eyes *.

"There were certainly some very beautiful details in it. But intolerable tediousness, innumerable repetitions, trifles uttered with pomp, unintelligible observations, opinions, and propositions, composed by far the greater part of it; not a principle, not one invulnerable assertion, not a single resource that might be expected from a statesman, not even one grand expedient becoming a financier, no plan of restoration, although such had been announced, no real *basis of stability*, albeit this was one of the divisions of the dis-

* In this third article, I have retrenched several paragraphs, containing observations on various particulars of the above-mentioned speech; they are less brilliant and less interesting than those which I have selected. W.

course;

course; and how should a man, who dares not talk of the constitution, create, and, above all, consolidate another order of things?

"His auditors were intoxicated with eagerness to applaud him, and they did applaud him till they were satiated.

"If it could be rendered consistent with decorum to bestow applause in a legislative assembly, there was one little bit which seemed to merit such an honour. It was that relative to bankruptcy: the director-general gave us the strongest and most honourable assurances, that there was no room for apprehension; and it were a grand source of consolation and security, if the means indicated by the minister, did not, for the most part, wound public credit, and endanger punctuality of payment.

"M. Necker moreover declared, that the

the king had recommended to him to give his sentiments in his name, *less as sovereign, than as the guardian of the interests of the nation.*

"Let us hope that the minister of the finances will at length understand, that it is now no longer time to pursue unsteady courses; that the current of public opinion is irresistible; that, if it do not aid him, it will sink him; that the reign of intrigue, like that of astrology*, is at an end; that cabal will perish at his feet, if he prove faithful to his principles, and will accomplish his rapid downfal, if he depart from them; that, strong in an unheard-of popularity, he hath nothing now to dread but the desertion of his own cause; and that if, in the situation in which the kingdom is plunged, an indefatigable patience

* Charlatanisme.

be neceffary, an inflexible fteadinefs is no lefs fo.

" Let us hope that the reprefentatives of the nation will henceforward entertain a more dignified idea of their functions, of their miffion, of their character; that they will not confent to act the part of enthufiafts, at any price, and upon every occafion; that, finally, inftead of exhibiting themfelves to Europe, in the light of fchool-boys juft efcaped from the ferula, and intoxicated with joy, becaufe they are promifed a week's holidays, they will fhew themfelves as men, and, as men, the flower of a nation, which, in order to be the firft on earth, requires nothing but a conftitution *.

* After admiring thefe paragraphs of Mirabeau, fo eloquent, fo full of wifdom, can our readers forbear exclaiming, in the words of his friend and editor,

tor, "The loss which France, which the world hath sustained, is immense, irreparable*!" The issue of revolutions often depends on a single citizen: *Thebes* rose and fell with *Epaminondas*. It were not altogether an ill-founded assertion, to say, that the French committed an important mistake, in so soon dissolving the first assembly, or, at least, in not reelecting the same men who had composed it. The impulse communicated to the original members, could not easily be transferred to their successors. It was something, to have been the fathers of the young constitution, to have hung over its cradle, to have assisted its infant efforts, and contracted for it that στοργη, that natural affection, which is the strongest of all ties, and the most durable. It was something to have known *Mirabeau*, to have been nourished by his instruction, to have been animated by his example, to have listened to him when his words made "their hearts burn within them."—I am afraid that those legislators, in their anxiety to avoid a new species of despotism, have done—what I hope they may never have reason to repent. W.

* See the preface to the first volume.

First

DECEMBER 10, 1789.

First Speech of M. de MIRABEAU, *in support of his motion for establishing a gradual progression in the elections to public offices.*

THE business relative to the municipalities was now finished, and the assembly, by repeated demonstrations of applause, had evinced to its committee of constitution, how well satisfied it was with their labours and their zeal.

MIRABEAU.

" THE proposition which I have the honour to submit to you, appears to me to contain an essential safe-guard of that constitution, which at this moment we are labouring to establish. The reception which

which you have afforded to moral confiderations, induces me to imagine, that your attention is ever obtainable, when matters of legiflation are prefented to you in that light.

" In the motion which I am laying before you, the queftion is, whether it be expedient to fubject to a gradual progreffion, the members of the different departments of the civil adminiftration? You perceive, gentlemen, that I have not been feduced by an ambition to become the parent of new and untried notions: it is in the practice of the beft regulated, the beft eftablifhed ftates, that I have difcovered traces of this law; but neither its antiquity, nor its fimplicity, will be, in your eyes, a reafon for rejecting it. It appears to me admirably adapted to that conftitution, which is the work of this affembly,

and

and to bind the several parts of it together.

"Had we not laid down equality as a fundamental law, it might perhaps be objected, that it is militating against the prejudices of certain individuals, to commence the career of office with a subaltern post; but, gentlemen, it behoves us to take heed, that this equality which we have sanctioned for a law, be not considered as an idle chimæra; it behoves us to take care, that it be traced, and retraced, through every branch of the constitution; that it become a principle which cannot be destroyed; and, as a consequence of our political establishments, that manners, customs, sentiments, should bear relation to the laws, as the laws relate to the model of reason and to the nature of things. If we neglect the secret causes of this concord, if we omit to place man in a state of harmony with the laws, we shall have formed a beauteous vision of philosophy, but we shall not have formed a constitution. The fundamental rules of good government are obvious; but to connect those rules so well with the execution, that obedience to the law may flow from the law itself, and inure the citizen to the yoke of law, by all the force of concurrent habits, is going far beyond philosophy, it is attaining the object of the legislator.

"Is not a gradual progress indicated by nature herself, in all her works, by the human mind in all its operations, by experience in all her maxims, as the progress to which the eternal Author of all beings hath thought it good and fitting to subject us? Politics are a science; administration is a
science

science and an art: but government embraces every thing that is great in human nature: the science, on which depends the destiny of states, is a second religion, both from its importance and its depth.

" Should, then, the most difficult of all arts, be the only one which we ought not to study? Must we look upon it in the same light in which we consider games of hazard, which one never attempts to learn, because they depend upon combinations beyond the reach of our sagacity? Must we reason upon politics, in a different mode from that, in which we reason upon all the other occupations of human life?

" If experience be not acquired but by degrees, if she extend her sphere by little and little, if the progress of nature be to rise in gradation from the simple to the compound, both nature and reason mean, that we should pass through the most simple functions of administration, before we arrive at those which are most complicated; that we should study the laws in their effects, and even in their action, before we obtain permission to reform them, and to dictate new laws; that, in fine, we should undergo a kind of trial, which removes all suspicion of incapacity or corruption, before we may be promoted to the great assembly of the nation *.

" I am now going to offer, in support of this system, some observations more particularly, and to answer a specious objection.

" Should you decree, gentlemen, that it shall be indispensable to have twice obtained the suffrages of the people, as a

---

* Something like this might remove the complaint in this kingdom, that too many of our senators assume that important character, while fresh from the birch of Eton and Westminster. W.

member of some administrative assembly, or some tribunal, in order to become eligible into the national assembly, you would stamp a double value upon elections of every kind, you would reduce those who look forward to offices, to the fortunate necessity of depending, from the very outset of their career, upon the esteem and goodwill of their fellow-citizens.

" I will be bold to say, that you would accomplish a revolution in the habits and manners of youth, who, at present, proceed from frivolity to corruption, from corruption to insignificance. The national elections would no longer be run away with, by cabal, by family-influence, by those prejudices invariably but too much favoured, in constitutions the most free; you would seem to say, by the decree which I propose: Whoever you be, do not flatter yourself that you shall carry every point, without having previously earned your honours by business and by services; you shall not advance, unless by justifying, at every step, the opinion of the public concerning you; you shall be weighed in the balance of experience, and unceasingly compared with your rivals. Interest may open the gates to you; but, while men who are as good as you, are slowly mounting every step of this instructive ladder, an indulgence mischievous to your own talents*, shall not lift you to

---

* Excellent!—How frequently do we see a stripling hurried, by his injudicious family, into Parliament, where

> " He struts and frets his hour upon the stage,
> " And then is heard no more,"

and who, had he been kept a little longer, might probably have risen to eminence. W.

the fummit, without your having given fome pledge for fo much confidence from the nation.

" Again, gentlemen: fuch a law would become a noble mean of preventing the degeneration of a clafs of men, who, in every part of the globe (with fome few exceptions, which are therefore the more honourable), feem to be abafed in the moral order, in proportion as they are elevated in that of civil fociety.

" The fecond motive, which, I declare, attracts me irrefiftibly towards the fyftem of gradation, is, the neceffity for rendering every public commiffion interefting and honourable, for diffufing an emulation of honour and virtue throughout the municipalities, for enhancing the value of popular fuffrages, even when they confer only a fubaltern employment.

"You will then no longer have any cause to fear, that the municipalities should be disdained by some, as situations beneath their acceptance, dreaded by others, as offices of fatigue and *ennui*, abandoned to a few candidates, who, destitute of all merit, of all ability, of all personal consequence, would in a little time make them cheap; for it frequently happens, that employments owe all their value, in the eyes of men, to the idea formed of those who seek for, or who occupy them.

"You know, gentlemen, that there is no post in society, be it ever so inconsiderable, which cannot confer lustre upon him who is without any, nor of ever so little profit, which presents not a resource, to the man who is unprovided. But we must exalt the municipalities, above the

reach

reach of the ambition and interests of candidates of this description.

"If the Romans had not concentred every thing within the walls of Rome, had they imparted a greater degree of splendour to the municipal administrations, had they made them the first step in the ladder of public honours, they would not have been obliged to make laws of restraint and rigour, in order to compel the inhabitants of the provincial towns to act in burthensome capacities. Those laws are yet in being; they bear witness to the errors of the masters of the world.

Let us avoid these errors; let us cherish our provinces; let us there diffuse a radiance round every employment, assigned by the suffrage of our country. Let us annihilate that unhappy prejudice, which, upon the ruins of our ancient distinctions,

would

would infallibly erect distinctions of another kind; which, upon the wreck of the classes and the orders, would create new classes, new orders, deriving their existence from the elections themselves, inevitable dissensions amongst the municipalities, the administrations of department, and the national assembly. We shall have done our duty but by halves, should we neglect to take away this dangerous resource from pride. But, we shall establish a kind of brotherhood amongst all the public functions, should the least important of those functions be made a necessary step to elevation; if the highest be connected, by indispensable transitions, with the lower degrees of office; should all public honours resemble a pure stream, distributed through different channels, but running one into another, perpetually limpid,

limpid, and, what is best of all, perpetually the same. This filiation of employments would produce another effect, no less " devoutly to be wished*;" the ambition of men would become, even in places of the lowest consequence, a security for the zealous execution of their duty. How powerful is that legislator, who hath discovered the secret of giving this moral direction to the passions, who hath succeeded in shewing the citizens their interest in their probity, who hath the happy talent of using their predominant inclinations, as so many mechanic powers for elevating the law †! Whatever function a person exercises, when it is only a transitory state of probation, in which his abilities, his integrity, are appreciated, with a view to his promotion to more important

* Non moins avantageux.
† Pour les leviers de la loi.

posts,

posts, from that moment you may rely on his unwearied attention to conduct himself irreproachably, and to conciliate the esteem of his fellow-citizens.

"You have framed wise regulations for securing the responsibility of every public officer; but to punish, to overawe, to restrain by dint of fear, is doing little: instead of whetting the subtilty and fatal industry of men, to counteract the laws by eluding them, we should fix their observation upon the motives, which, penetrating to the bottom of the heart, render obedience both agreeable and easy. Severe laws have no other effect, than to force from us a deceitful and degenerate submission: but honour, placed as a deposit in the suffrages of the people; but hope, dexterously managed from post up to post, and from function up to function;

tion *; but ambition, invited to deserve every thing, where, before, she usurped every thing,—these, gentlemen, are secret springs, the power of which is proportioned to the obstacles to be surmounted, springs so tempered, that liberty herself must perish, ere that temper can be destroyed†.

" I rest with confidence upon an authority, respectable in the eyes of every one, who is a friend to the public good. The immortal author‡ of the Social Contract hath, on very many occasions, be-

---

* De place en place, et de fonction en fonction.

† Des ressorts qui ont la trempe indestructible de la liberté.

‡ Rousseau. A great man, had he confined himself to politics and romances, and forborne to trifle with Christianity. W.

stowed

stowed the highest praises on the system of gradation, which I have the honour to lay before you. In the glorious days of Rome, says he, they passed through the prætorship, in order to arrive at the consulate. Integrity, adds the same author, could not be carried to a higher pitch, than it was amongst the quæstors of the Roman armies, since the quæstorship was the first step towards attaining the curule magistracies.

"It will not be useless to observe, that, in the system of gradation, offices, otherwise obscure, become ennobled by the perspective of those which are more elevated: men naturally mount upwards to the level of their hopes. Would you animate every portion of the kingdom; would you dignify even the meanest employments; let services be the only road to advancement,
and

and let every public ftation be preparatory to fome other.

" But, it will be faid, we are going to trefpafs on the freedom of elections. We have laid it down as a principle, that they ought to depend on confidence alone, and we are going to prefcribe limits to confidence.—I do not believe, gentlemen, that this objection is well founded.

" To fix on a certain meafure of fortune, or on a certain degree of birth, and fet it up as the condition of eligibility, is ftriking at all thofe who belong not to this league, is pronouncing their exclufion, is difinheriting them of their natural right; but, to attach to the progrefs of promotion rules which equally extend to all, which leave to all the fame rights, the fame hopes, which are pointed againft privileges in favour of equality, is not wounding the

principle,

principle, it is acting as its protector and guardian.

"What, then? shall the unlimited principle of the freedom of election, extend to the condemnation of those very laws, which we have adopted from free states, for the purpose of securing the transition of employments, of compelling the renovation of them, after a certain number of years! Shall this principle condemn the laws, which fix the age of majority civil and political! But if the object of the law hath been, to be assured of the experience and judgment of those who aspire to public offices, since judgment and experience depend less on length of life, than on the use that one hath made of it, the requiring a noviciate, in order to become eligible into the legislative body, is entering thoroughly into the spirit of that law.

"I be-

" I beseech you, gentlemen, to make, with respect to confidence, an observation peculiar to a representative government, such as ours.

" We are elected by a single department, and we become the representatives of the whole kingdom. We are not even elected by all the citizens of a department; but by a small number of delegates from amongst them.

" Hence, in my opinion, results a truth, which cannot be controverted, and that is, that the confidence which the legislative body is to enjoy, were precarious, if means were not discovered of doubling it, in some measure.

" Observe how much broader a basis you are giving to confidence, by making it thus bear upon the system of gradual election; we shall have nothing to apprehend from the first choice of seduced electors, of electors imposed upon, perhaps corrupted; but every choice they make shall be justified beforehand, by the proofs shewn by the candidate, both of his talents and his virtues. Such elections are likely to be by so much the more popular, as a greater number of citizens will have participated, directly or indirectly, in the appointment of the members of the National Assembly.

" The electors may then say to their fellow-citizens: Our choice hath been directed by yours; we do not present you with an unknown man. His services have gone before him like a herald*, and the voice of the public hath recommended him to our favour.

" As for the provinces, they will, by these means, give one another mutual se-

---
* Il est précédé de ses services.

curities,

curities, that neither cabal, nor interest, nor complaisance, nor venality, nor popular caprice, nor sudden whim, shall abandon the fate of the empire to corrupt or silly representatives. Thus shall the provinces experience a more profound calm, more perfect tranquillity, upon the faith of public reason; the sovereign decrees shall meet with more respect, and moral opinion shall become their best authority.

" To establish confidence on a more solid foundation, is not making an attempt to injure her: no objection, then, should be started against the system of gradation, upon the ground of one of its greatest advantages.

" Should the moral and political considerations, which I have just now laid before you, determine you to sanction this experimental and gradual progress, it will be be expedient to appoint a time at which it shall take place, and from which it shall be rigidly obferved. To ordain that it shall commence immediately, were to defire an impoffibility; but in the fpace of eight or ten years, the number of citizens who shall have paffed through the municipalities, the tribunals, the departments, or this affembly, will form fuch a fund of able candidates, as will prefent an immenfe field to the electors.

" I move you to come to the following refolutions:

" 1. That, from the firft day of January, 1797, no perfon shall be capable of being elected member of the National Affembly, unlefs he have been honoured, at leaft twice, with the fuffrages of the people, as member of fome adminiftrative affemblies of department, of diftrict, or of
the

the municipalities; or unless he have filled, during three years at least, an office of magistracy; or, in fine, unless he have been once already a member of the National Assembly.

"2. From the year 1795, no person shall be elected member of the assemblies of department, unless he have already executed functions in the assemblies of district, or in the municipalities.

"3. And, in order that the laws relating to these points, may not require too advanced an age in the candidate, every active citizen shall be eligible to municipal employments, as soon as he shall have attained the age of twenty-one years."

The assembly listened to this discourse with a degree of attention, expressive of their opinion of the importance of a question, at once so new and so interesting.

However, as soon as the first article was read, the discontents manifested by some interrupted the reading of the remainder. M. de Mirabeau in vain declared, that the three articles composed but one. *You will have sufficient time*, added he, *for demonstrating their perverse and wicked meaning**. It was not till after a considerable interval, that he finished the reading of the decree, and that one could judge by the applause given, that the Assembly was at least divided in opinion.

He had scarce descended from the tribune, when M. Barnave took his place.

"If," said he, "in order to annihilate the constitution, at a single blow, it were sufficient to envelop, in some moral ideas,

* These words are a strong proof, that Mirabeau knew what weapons his enemies might employ against him.

and

and some scraps of erudition, principles the most opposite to the declaration of rights, and to our decrees, the member who spoke last might flatter himself that he had produced that effect upon you; but, fortunately, he hath armed you against the seduction of his eloquence; and often have we been obliged to seek for reason and the public good, amidst that multitude of elegancies, with which he usually embellishes his sentiments. This necessity appears to-day in a manner still more striking."

And then M. Barnave attacked the motion upon these grounds:

1. It was contradictory to several decrees, and retarded for several years, the time appointed for admission to public offices.

2. It tended to unite, in a small number

of perfons, the municipal, adminiftrative, and legiflative powers.

3. Men, who, by their ftudies, might have fitted themfelves for a place in the National Affembly, would find themfelves under the neceffity of paffing through employments, for which they were not at all adapted.

And, after having promulgated thefe three mighty motives, for reprobating the project, M. Barnave thus expreffed himfelf:

" The conclufion which I am to draw, hath been already provided for me by the member who fpoke laft. I do not conceive, how any one can propofe to a nation, to make a law which cannot be executed in lefs than ten years: I know not whether even that term would prove fufficient. You will have occafion, fome

year

year or other, for a national convention, for the purpofe of rectifying the errours, which experience fhall have fhewn to exift in the conftitution. I move you that the motion be adjourned to the time of that convention."

M. MIRABEAU.

" The member who fpoke laft, appears to have forgotten, that, though rhetoricians talk to anfwer the purpofe of a day, the legiflator's difcourfe is directed to futurity. I afk leave to reply to him; but, as I am fummoned to attend the committee of ten*, I quit the affembly, in order to repair whither it commands me; and I requeft that the debate be adjourned†."

The debate was adjourned.

DECEM-

---

* Appointed to examine different plans of finance.

† In what, then, it will be afked, confifts the fault

of

December 15, 1789.

The motion of Mirabeau, upon the system of gradation, was the order of the day.

It of this motion of Mirabeau?—In this—Henceforward, something more shall be requisite, to entitle a candidate to be elected a legislator, than pronouncing from some tribune, or in the middle of the streets, these grand words, PEOPLE, LIBERTY, EQUALITY, REGENERATION, SALVATION OF THE KINGDOM, ABHORRENCE OF TYRANTS. It shall be necessary to have proved, that the candidate loves the *people* for its sake, and not for his own; that the prime object of his love, is the *liberty* of all, and not his own exclusively; that he cherishes *equality* by so much the more, as he never entertained a wish to be himself the head, or even the member of an imperious tribe, which separates itself by proud distinctions from the rest of the community*; that he

possesses

---

* D'une caste impératiye et isolée.—We have no such word as *isolated*, at least in authors of good authority. W.

It had scarcely been mentioned, when M. Verchère called for the question of adjournment.

M. *Clermont-Tonnerre* was for debating it.

M. *Rœderer* was of the same opinion. " One of the reasons," said he, "upon which M. Mirabeau founds his motion, is to render respectable in the eyes of every citizen, such offices as are the first step in the scale of administration. Many, fitted to fill stations in the municipalities, will possess not only the courage, but likewise the ability, to co-operate in bringing about a *regeneration* which is indispensable; that he hath the virtue to sacrifice, to *the salvation of the kingdom*, his very ambition, nay, even his self-love; that, in fine, he not only *abhors tyrants*, but that he likewise feels no tendency to become a tyrant himself.—It is evident, that all this is difficult to be proved, and doubtless, the easiest way is, to stifle the difficulty of the proof.

despise

despise them, should those stations be separated from the other public employments. When considering them as a ladder to the superior posts, they will immediately press forward to occupy them, although the effect of the motion is not to take place until the year 1797: consequently, I am of opinion that the motion ought not to be adjourned.

M. Mirabeau the younger said: What good citizen should stand in need of the hope of arriving at superior place, to prevail on him to fill a post where he can be useful to his country? Such a good citizen were an intriguing &c.

M. Duport was for the adjournment.

M. MIRABEAU.

" When I beheld a member mount the tribune, with a readiness which I admired as much as I well could, for the purpose of attacking, unpreparedly, a motion which I had the conscience to meditate maturely, and which stood propped upon the opinion of Rousseau, that is, of the man who most reflected upon the state of human affairs, I should have needed only to repeat myself, in order to reply to him.

" I was summoned several times by one of your committees, and I desired that the debate should be adjourned.

" When I heard it proposed, that the question should be adjourned to the year 1797, I thought that nothing more was meant than a stroke of pleasant raillery: in fact, this is the first time that an attempt hath ever been made, to prevent legislators from extending their views into futurity.

" It hath already been observed, that, to form

form a constitution, is to labour for the time to come, is to foresee, is to determine long beforehand, the manners, the opinions, the habitudes of a nation. If the law which I propose, be as the key-stone of the arch, if it connect the several parts by one common point of union, you ought not to defer sanctioning it, although its execution be necessarily retarded. Imagine not that it remains even as a *pierre d'attente**: its influence will begin to operate immediately, both on those who look forward to a share in public business, who will not despise the municipal employments, and on the electors, who will confer, with a more scrupulous choice, such offices as are most desirable, and on

* A corner-stone left jutting out from a building, in order to be afterwards connected with another edifice.

the administrations themselves, which will be looked upon as a state of probation.

"The member who attacked my motion would be very much embarrassed, were he asked, whether, when only an ensign in the regiment wherein he distinguished himself*, he never aspired to the commission which he hath at present the honour to bear. I know not for what description of men it can be true, that emulation is the same with intrigue; I know not in what class of angelic beings, the desire of doing good is the only desire existing: such perfection is not made for this world.

" I do not think it becoming the wisdom and justice of the Assembly, to prevent me from answering objections, that have pro-

* Lorsqu'il servoit dans le premier grade où il portoit les armes avec distinction.

duced

duced an effect upon my motion, which I flatter myself I am able to destroy. If the adjournment be to any fixed period, I will not suffer a murmur to escape me; but if it be indefinite, I must say, that a law, which is sanctioned by the authority of the first genius of the age, and which even its enemies acknowledge to have a very moral tendency, is treated with an indecorum, highly unworthy of this assembly.

"That I may enjoy the benefit of the order of the day, I ask leave to answer the objections. Should I do it in such a manner as to crush all further debate upon the subject *, you will pronounce your decision; should the question appear to you not sufficiently explained, you will discuss it, or you will adjourn it."

* D'une manière péremptoire.

The Assembly came to two resolutions; first, to adjourn the motion, and then, to adjourn it indefinitely.

The honour of decreeing the moral proposition of M. Mirabeau, is reserved, then, for a second legislature; let us hope that that legislature, will make it a point of conscience and of zeal, to give it the full authority of law.

DECEMBER 29, 1789.

On the morning of the 18th, the Assembly had taken cognizance of a letter addressed to M. Necker, by M. Tronchin, in the name of the city of Geneva.

In this letter, M. Necker was, in the first place, made acquainted with the penury of the Genevans, and, in the next, commissioned to offer to the National Assembly, fembly, in the name of the republic, a gift of nine hundred thoufand livres, to be paid out of the life-annuities of the year 1789.

M. *de Volney* had faid : " It is very evident, that the government of Geneva does not owe its exiftence to the free confent of the nation, but is merely fupported by us as guarantees. If we may credit certain reports, which feem to merit our attention, this generofity is far from being gratuitous. It is connected by fome thread, which we may come at, with the guaranty juft ratified in favour of the party of the Genevan ariftocrates, in oppofition to the interefts of the republic. This Affembly, by accepting a pretended gratuity, would appear, and it ought not to appear, to protect engagements contrary to every principle of liberty."

In confequence of thefe judicious obfervations,

servations, which were felt by every true friend to freedom, the question, whether the nine hundred thousand livres should be accepted, had been adjourned.

On this day, M. *de Volney*, beginning the debate on the acceptation, read the following paragraph of a letter, which had been addressed to him by certain citizens of Geneva:

Extract of a letter from Messrs. Claviere, du Roveray, and Dumont, to M. Volney.

"We will not say that this gift, an-
"nounced by the Genevans as the effect
"of their particular regard for M. Necker,
"is, either the price of his civility, or a
"condition, without which the guaranty,
"granted to them by government, was
"not to hold good; but we affirm, as
"facts notorious in Geneva, that the last
"assurances

"assurances given by M. Necker to the magistrates of this city, with respect to obtaining the guaranty, agree, in point of time, with the invitation made to them in his name, to interest themselves in *the patriotic contribution*:—that the subscriptions relative to that matter, commenced almost at the same juncture;—that they remained open, till the arrival of the full powers, by virtue of which the guaranty was signed;—and that it was then only, that the final result of the subscription was addressed to that minister."

M. *de Volney* concluded with advising, that the offer should be rejected.

M. *Toulongeon* said: "Why should it be supposed that the Genevans had any other motive, than that of contributing their share towards the re-establishment

of

of our finances, since their whole fortune is inseparably connected with our prosperity, and our calamity would bring on their ruin?"

MIRABEAU.

"This cannot be considered as a gratuity; their letter is sufficient to teach us the true value of their motives: I will not at present talk of probabilities, I will only comment upon what they themselves have written: you see there but too much to confirm you in that distrust, which, by an instinct of liberty, you felt at the very moment when this offering was announced to you.

"What is the nature of this gift? It is not a patriotic contribution. The Genevans have long enjoyed the honour of having a country of their own. It is an act of their generosity, it is a philanthropic succour, it is, say they, *a precious opportunity which ought to be seized, because it may never come again* *, of testifying their *respect*, their *devotion*, their *gratitude to a beneficent king, to a generous nation, who have, at all times, interested themselves in the welfare of the republic.* It is not here, then, that we find that contribution, which is the object of our decree; and nothing can be less like even the quarter of their revenues, than these nine hundred thousand livres which are offered to us, since Geneva possesses, in France, annuities to the amount of at least twelve or fifteen millions.

" Who are the donors? another consideration, which goes beyond mere curiosity. They who have signed that let-

* Une occasion precieuse et unique à saisir.

ter, are precisely Genevan aristocrates, that is, the very persons who have indefatigably endeavoured to suspend the sword of foreign interference, over the heads of their fellow-citizens. Yes, gentlemen, they are all aristocrates, two excepted, who belong to the popular party, and who may have been imposed upon, as a member who hath already spoken, remarked. But, furthermore, they are all, without exception, members of that government, of that unremovable body which is no longer elected by the people, and which, in 1782, took possession of all the rights of the sovereign assembly, like unnatural children who would bar out* their father, with a view of usurping his estate.

" The letter of the donors informs us,

* Interdire.

that the persons who have signed it are members of a committee, appointed by the subscribers to forward to you their gift.

"I cannot perceive the effect of chance, in the composition of this committee; but I perceive in it the intentions of the government, which, without acting of itself, is desirous of being confounded with its members; and I perceive them still better, in the solemnity of the gift, in the intervention of the republic's agent, and in that of the minister of the finances.

"And at what juncture is this gift presented to you? It agrees as precisely, in point of time, with the guaranty which they obtained, as if it were the price and the compensation for that guaranty. These suspicions are corroborated, when we find, in the letter of the donors, that,

far

far from being the surplus of abundance, this present is a sacrifice snatched from indigence and necessity. Singular generosity! What? the citizens of Geneva see around them a people, connected with them by the strongest relations, by the ties of blood, by the social and patriotic affections; they are witnesses of their want, they themselves draw us a lugubrious picture of it; and, at a time when their beneficence can and ought to be exercised in favour of their brethren, they prefer scattering it abroad, dispatching it to distant places *, preceded by the trumpet of renown; they offer us a magnificent present set in misery †. They forget, that our delicacy would induce us rather to offer relief to them, and that at

* De l'envoyer au loin.
† Dans le cadre de la misère.

least

least we might say: Arouse the languid arts, support your manufactures, invite plenty into your laps, before you dream of offering us presents, which humanity would not suffer us to accept, unless with this condition, of showering them back with usury upon your famishing fellow-citizens*.

[*Here thunders of applause from every quarter of the Assembly.*]

" Every one of these reflections originates in the very letter of the donors: but what events should I have to describe, were I to sound the depths of that *beneficence*, of that *interest which we have at all times taken in the welfare of the republic*, and which animate the gratitude of the Genevan aristocrates! It were neces-

* *Bravo!*—Que pour les reverser avec usure sur les indigens de votre patrie.

sary

sary to display before you the citizens of Geneva, in 1766, wrestling with the pride and despotism of M. de Choiseul, who, in order to tread them down, and punish them for their noble love of liberty, wreaked his vengeance on them by menaces, by laying their commerce under an interdict, by a *cordon* of troops which shut them up within their walls. It were necessary to represent to you Geneva, in 1782, besieged, usurped, the defenders of the people banished, the people itself disarmed, treated like a conquered enemy, subjected to the double yoke of military and civil despotism, and five hundred citizens of Geneva fleeing with horror from their oppressed country. Such, gentlemen, are the services which we have done the Genevan aristocrates; such the benefits for which they are now repaying us.

us. But the moment is not yet come, for agitating the question respecting national guaranties, for examining whether we shall leave ministers the power of entangling France, in the internal disturbances of other countries, of sowing the seeds of future difficulties, wars, expences, burthensome to us, absurd in themselves, and odious to all our neighbours.

"That question will be brought before you by the Genevans themselves, who, at the very time when their government was soliciting the guaranty, began to unite, yet slowly, for the purpose of asking your leave to be as free in their own country, as you are desirous of being here. You will then, gentlemen, have an opportunity of knowing what these guaranties, these pretended benefits, have done both for Geneva and France.

"To

" To Geneva, they have proved a copious and continual fource of troubles and diftractions, from the year 1738.

" To France, they have produced a feries of blunders, of faults, of acts which difhonoured the nation, were it poffible for us to be accountable for what our minifters, or their dull commiffaries, did, in the name of the nation, when the nation was confidered as nothing.

" This hateful labyrinth of intrigues and injuries, will, fooner or later, be fubmitted to your infpection; and it will be for you to decide, whether fuch guaranties be confiftent with morality and the rights of nations.

" It is for you now to eftimate the magnitude and the nature, of the gift which is prefented to you, and the purity of the motives which led to fuch an offering.

" I move

"I move you to come to the following resolutions:

"That the president shall return for answer to the first minister of the finances:

"That the National Assembly, deeply
"affected by the distressed state of the
"arts, the commerce, and the manufac-
"tures of Geneva, and likewise by the
"extravagantly high price of corn, men-
"tion of which is made in the letter
"communicated by the minister, is of
"opinion, that the nine hundred thousand
"livres, which are offered to it in that
"letter, would be applied with more pro-
"priety, if employed in relieving the Ge-
"nevans themselves, and that, conse-
"quently, it hath come to a resolution
"not to accept them."

[*Fresh applause bore witness, that M. de
Mirabeau had completely met the opinion of the Assembly.*]

After having heard the Abbé Maury, whose sentiments coincided with those of M. Mirabeau, it was resolved, most unanimously, that the offer of the Genevans should be rejected, and that the president should communicate the said resolution to the first minister of the finances.

JANUARY 22, 1790.

Speech upon the motion for expelling the Abbé Maury, who had made use of expressions offensive to the Assembly.

During a debate on a report made by the committee of finances, upon some business relating to the liquidation of the public debt, the Abbé Maury had behaved in such a manner, as to incur the displeasure of the Assembly. Without troubling

troubling the reader with the debate itself, and the several amendments proposed, I take up the affair of the Abbé Maury at the following paragraph of the French editor.

The plan of the decree is read.

The Abbé Maury darts into the tribune, declaims against that part of the Assembly, which would fain, says he, obstruct the verification of the debt (no soul had thought of it), and addressed it in these words *à la Brebeuf**: " I desire that those men, to whom nature hath refused the least spark of courage, and to whom she hath given no other recompense than shame, may answer me in this Assembly—"

Here the orator is interrupted, and, amidst symptoms of disapprobation the

* Some person, probably, whose style resembled that of the Abbé.

M. MIRABEAU.

"The vexatious incident which troubles this debate, affords you an ample proof that choler is an evil counsellor: for the member who hath just had the misfortune to offend you, hath directly counteracted the success of his opinion, which was actually triumphant, at the moment when he stood up as its defender. Let us imitate neither his violence, nor his want of dexterity. Let us be calm, since we are about to perform the office of judges. But, gentlemen, before I give my sentiments, as to the conduct which it behoves you to pursue in the present case, allow me to request the president, to state exactly the point for deliberation."

Here the flame breaks out again with redoubled fury; one fide of the hall calls for the expulfion of the Abbé Maury; M. Guillaume declares himfelf the author of the motion, and perfifts in requiring, that the prefident be authorized to write to Péronne, to the conftituents of the Abbé, for the purpofe of requefting them to recall their deputy.

Mirabeau wifhes to be heard, but is oppofed by M. Montlaufier, who takes upon him to foretell, that M. Mirabeau is about to make fome very violent motion.

M. MIRABEAU.

" Had I not been interrupted by the member who fpoke laft, he might already have known, that it is more fatisfactory*

* Plus fimp'e.

to listen than to divine, and that, in general, the trade of prophecy is far from being an unerring one. It is already evident, that I have not affronted the understanding* of this assembly, by desiring the president should state the proposition, upon which I was going to deliberate. In the first moments of that indignation, which so naturally seized the assembly, your ears were struck, gentlemen, with the word *expulsion*; I saw started, on a sudden, a grand question of public right, which certainly is neither decided, nor reduced into proper form; and as, in this universal ferment, it might be prejudged in a manner highly mortifying, I have ascended the tribune, in order to endeavour to prevent such prejudication. It is so painful to rise to speak, when one hath no

* Desservi la raison.

opinion to give but what bears hard upon a colleague, that no other motive whatever fhould have fwayed me. But I confidered it my duty, to warn the juftice of this affembly, and to remind it, that, ere the expulfion of a member be decreed, it becomes us to inquire whether we poffefs the right, and that the prefent circumftance is not favourable to a difcuffion of fuch folemnity. A few moments have proved fufficient to fhew M. Guillaume, that it was more conformable to the principle, which at leaft is not difputed, to confine himfelf to a declaration of the prefumed incapacity of the Abbé Maury, by requefting his conftituents to nominate another deputy; and this very fevere fentence, gentlemen, you moft unqueftionably have a right to adopt.

" I would obferve, however, that if
the

the passionate behaviour of the Abbé Maury can neither be justified nor suffered, it yet carries with it a species of excuse. Undoubtedly the Abbé Maury was not himself, when he spoke in a manner so injudicious. His culpable apostrophe was directed to no particular person, who can be named as the intended object. Had he meant it for the assembly at large, it were a kind of sacrilegious phrenzy, which perhaps ought to subject him only to the punishment due to madmen. Had he named any of us, it would have been incumbent on you to procure satisfaction to the insulted member; but nothing like this was the case. The fact committed by the Abbé Maury, was only a scandalous burst of passion, which, in my opinion, merits only a chastisement of simple discipline; and my advice, therefore, is, that the Abbé Maury be censured, and that the censure be recorded on the journals. Sir [*addressing himself to M. de Mont-lausier*], should you have guessed at this conclusion?"

The Abbé Maury now ascends the tribune, attempts to justify himself, but with an aukwardness very unconciliating; at length he calls upon M. Mirabeau, to mention in what particular *his mode of reasoning had been absurd, and his expressions injurious.*

M. MIRABEAU.

" I might decline speaking of *the absurdity* of the mode of reasoning, since that is not the count upon which the Abbé Maury is indicted, and because it appears to me, that every one is at full liberty, to talk as absurdly as he can and as he pleases.

pleafes. However, in order to anfwer the challenge juft given me, I will fay, that I thought it *an abfurdity,* to conclude that, becaufe the affembly was inclined to verify the *non-conftituted* debt, it was not inclined to verify the debt which was conftituted, and alfo, to make an outrageous declamation upon an imaginary opinion, which no perfon in this affembly had fuggefted.

" With refpect to what I find *injurious* in the expreffions of the Abbé Maury, I am forry that he compels me to mention them again; but I fhall do it briefly, and with fimplicity.

" Had the Abbé Maury confined himfelf to this part of what he uttered: *I defire that thofe men, to whom nature hath refufed the leaft fpark of courage, and whom fhe hath not even recompenfed by fhame,* it might

might be contended, that that was only a figure of rhetoric, inapplicable, and in a bad taste; but these words, *that they may answer me*, even though one were to separate them from the rest, as he would fain do with these words, *in this assembly*, are a direct and pointed apostrophe, and, consequently, it is utterly impossible to justify them. Now, we understood them so clearly, at least in that part of the hall where I was seated, that we all cried out: *It is for the Abbé Maury alone, to ask the question and to answer it.*

"But, gentlemen, this whole debate is so austere, and so indignant*, that God forbid I should prolong it by unnecessary reflections. In my mind, it were for the interest of even the Abbé Maury himself, to curtail it, and I doubt that his apology,

* Si triste et si fastidieux.

adorned

adorned by *the roaring of rage**, will conduce to make my opinion be considered as too severe, an opinion in which I persist."

The debate was lengthened out still further; but, at last, it was resolved, that the Abbé Maury should be censured, and that the censure should be recorded on the journals.

* The Abbé, amongst other things which he had said in his justification, had given vent to these expressions: *A man who mounts the tribune without any preparation, and who is incessantly interrupted by the roaring of rage*——Here he was overpowered by the clamours of the assembly.

Speech on the propofition for annulling the imperative mandates, and for fixing the renewal of the Affembly, after completing the conftitution.

The powers of fome of the deputies were on the point of expiration, as their commiffions were limited to a year.

It became neceffary to provide againft, to prevent, the diforganization of the Affembly.

The committee of conftitution propofed to decree; 1. That the National Affembly could not be renewed, until the conftitution were completed; 2. That the commiffions of the deputies were null and void, with refpect to the duration of the exifting feffion.

This propofal found a violent opponent in

in the Abbé Maury. But the Abbé Maury spoke for a long time, and said nothing. The hackneyed argument, *that the deputies were the deputies of the bailiwicks, before they became those of the nation*, and that, *consequently*, they owed obedience to their constituents, was exhibited under a thousand different forms, and, nevertheless, the friends of the Abbé Maury were the only members who considered it as conclusive.

MIRABEAU.

" I cannot, without the deepest indignation, hear ill-minded declaimers incessantly oppose the nation in the National Assembly, and make efforts to excite a sort of rivalship between them; as if it were not by the exertions of the National Assembly, that the nation hath discovered, recovered,

re-

re-acquired all her rights! as if it were not by the exertions of the National Affembly, that the French, until then an unconftituted aggregation of difunited tribes, are truly become a nation! as if, encompaffed by the monuments of our labours, of our dangers, of our fervices, we could become the objects of public fufpicion, and formidable to the liberties of the people! as if, while the eyes of the two worlds are fixed upon you, the fortunate enthufiafm* of a great revolution, the grand fpectacle of your glory, the gratitude of fo many millions, even the pride of a generous confcioufnefs, which fhame would not fuffer to belie itfelf, were not a fufficient pledge, for your fidelity, your patriotifm, and your virtue!

* Le fanatifme heureux.—*Fanatifme* is a bad word to be applied in fuch a fenfe. W.

" A mem-

"A member who hath already spoken, hath, in combating with great art the system of the committee, defined the national convention to be, a nation assembled by proxy*, for the purpose of giving itself a government. This definition is manifestly very inaccurate, or very incomplete. Eh! why might not a nation, which can form a convention for the purpose of giving itself a government, with equal reason form one, in order to change, to modify, to reform the existing government? Undoubtedly, the Abbé Maury will not deny that the French, assembled in convention, would not possess, for instance, the right of augmenting the royal prerogative.

"The same member hath asked, how, from simple deputies of bailiwicks, we

* Une nation assemblée par ses repréfentans.

were

were suddenly transformed into a national convention? I will answer him:—On the day, when, finding the hall, where by right we should have assembled, shut up, surrounded, polluted by a forest of bayonets*, we ran to the first place which could receive us, and there took an oath to perish, sooner than suffer the then order of things to subsist; on that same day, if we were not one before, did we become a national convention. The deputies of the people formed a national convention, when despotism, by an act of frenzy truly sacrilegious, attempted to hinder them from fulfilling their sacred mission; they formed a national convention, for the purpose of putting an end to arbitrary power, and of defending, from all violence, the rights of the French nation.

* Fermée, herissée, fouillée de baïonnettes.

You perceive, gentlemen, that I despise craft, that I disdain all subtilties; it is not by metaphysical distinctions, that I attack particular oaths, oaths taken indiscreetly or rashly, oaths of which the National Assembly will not judge, of which it does not become her to take cognizance. I will not even avail myself of all my advantages; I will not ask whether, being commissioned to frame a constitution, we have not been empowered by that very circumstance, to do every thing that might be necessary to the finishing, the establishing, the fortifying that constitution; whether the instructions which gave in charge to us the *regeneration* of France, did not thereby confer on us unlimited powers, as to that object; whether the king himself have not pronounced this word *regeneration*, and thereby admitted all its consequences;

sequences; whether, in the circumstances attending the revolution, and by which we have been agitated, we could, we ought to have interrogated our constituents, lost in cowardly consultations the invaluable time for action, and left our infant liberty to be struck with a death's wound, in order to satisfy the scruples of the numerous host of proselytes, with which all established authority is surrounded. I say, that, let our powers have been what they might, at the juncture, when, convoked by lawful authority, we assembled in one great body, they changed their nature on the 20th of June, because that change was necessary to the salvation of our country; that, if they had need of any extension, they acquired it on that memorable day, when, wounded in our dignity, in our rights, in our duties,

ties, we bound ourselves to provide for public safety, by the oath never to separate, till the constitution should be fixed upon the basis of stability *.

"The wicked attempts of despotism, the perils which we have charmed †, the violence that we have subdued, are the titles by which we sit here; they have been sanctioned by our success; the reiterated adherence of every part of the empire, hath given them the stamp of law, hath sanctified them.

"Let those who have cast upon us the strange reproach, of having used new words, to express new sentiments and principles, new ideas and institutions, now seek, in the vain vocabulary of vulgar things, the definition of the words, *national con-*

* Ne fût établie et affirmie.
† Que nous avons conjurés.

vention. Called forth by the alarm-bell of neceffity, the loud and awful peals of which no clamour can overcome*, our national convention is above all imitation, as it is above all authority; it is accountable to itfelf alone, and can be judged but by pofterity (1).

"Gentlemen, you are all acquainted with that fublime trait in the character of that Roman, who, in order to fave his country from the effects of a vile confpiracy, had been obliged to exceed the powers entrufted to him by the laws. A captious tribune required him, to fwear that he had refpected the laws; hoping, by this infidious propofal, to reduce the conful to the dilemma, of either in-

---

* Provoqués par l'invincible tocfin de la néceffité.
(1) *Bravo!*

curring

curring the guilt of perjury, or of making an embarrassing declaration: *I swear*, said that great man, *I swear that I have saved the republic.* Gentlemen,—I swear that you have been the saviours of your country—."

Few speeches have produced more effect, than that which I have just reported. The applause was loud and reiterated.

The plan of the committee was passed into a law.

May 15, 1790.

On the 14th, the president received a letter from M. de Montmorin, minister for foreign affairs, informing him that, in consequence of certain warlike preparations then carrying on in England, his majesty had

had thought fit to order an armament of fourteen ſhips of the line, in the ports of the Mediterranean, the Ocean, &c.

The debate upon this letter took place on the following day.

M. *de Biron* ſpoke firſt. It was his opinion, that the king ſhould be thanked, for the meaſures which he had taken for the preſervation of peace, and invited to lay before the aſſembly the wants of the marine department.

M. *Alexandre de Lameth* obſerved, that the queſtion ariſing from the letter of the miniſter, ſuppoſed the deciſion of another, which the aſſembly had, as yet, not thought proper to diſcuſs; namely, whether the right of making war and peace, belonged to the people or to the king.— He thought, that, previous to coming to any reſolution upon the meaſures taken by by the king, with respect to the English armament, it was necessary to pronounce upon the constitutional question, which he had intimated to the assembly.

The opinion of this last speaker was supported by Messieurs Barnave, Broglie, and Robertspierre—opposed by Messieurs Duport and Goupil.

MIRABEAU.

"I mean not to speak yet, with regard to the message in question, although I have made up my mind upon that subject. I shall examine, whether the constitutional question be entitled to a previous discussion. I request that my opinion be not prejudged. This mode of eluding the question, to which the letter of the minister hath given rise, is unreasonable, inconclusive, imprudent, and without object. I say that it is unreasonable and inconclusive, because the message of the king might exist, even though we should have determined, that to the nation belongs the right of making war or peace. The right of arming, of suddenly putting himself in a posture of defence, will ever be the right of the supreme executor of the nation. Allow me to make use of an ordinary expression: the *maréchaussée* external and internal, by sea and by land, ought always, considering the emergency of a case of sudden danger, to be placed in the hands of the king. I say, again, that this mode of eluding the decision is inconclusive, because it were going on the supposition, that the order issued by the king for the armament, is illegal.

" Certain it is, that in every society, the

the provisional is in force until the definitive be determined: now, the king hath the provisional; therefore, he might legally give orders for an armament. I say, in the next place, that this mode of eluding the question, is not prudent. Supposing, that, in fact, the previous discussion of the question of right were necessary, our debate would occasion delays, which would furnish a pretext for saying, that we had obstructed the measures taken to insure public tranquillity, and the safety of our commerce. I admit, that the right of making peace or war should be discussed incontinently, and I move for an adjournment, the shortest that can well be. But, undoubtedly, this great question ought necessarily to be prepared beforehand, by the committee of constitution; it involves many other questions.—Is it possible that you wish to suspend the debate upon the king's message? Are you not well aware, that the supplies are unprovided for? Are you not well aware, that twenty-four ships, armed merely because England was arming, can be to you no object of apprehension?

"The extraordinary aid demanded from you, is, gentlemen, but too necessary; it is not dangerous. Would not a refusal expose you to the murmurs and resentment of the merchants? But too many means are employed already to excite such discontent. To thank the king for the measures which he hath taken for the preservation of peace, is exhibiting to the nation the armament in the light of a grand precaution; it is the way to beget confidence in every heart. But, if you go to tell the people, that you must suspend

pend all your labours, in order to learn to whom belongs the right of making war or peace, the people will say in return: Precautions are not the only point in question, the war is ready to burst upon our heads.

" Thus it is that public affairs are injured and undone, by disseminating idle apprehensions. Were ministerial manœuvres fraught with *nation-slaying* projects*, it were, at most, a conspiracy of pigmies; no person can imagine, that fourteen ships put into commission, are an object capable of frightening the constitution. Though the constitutional question were decided, the king might do what he hath done; he might take such measures as it became him to take, saving

* *Nation-homicides.*—Mirabeau hath coined the word, and his translator must counterfeit it.

the

the eternal responsibility of ministers. You cannot, therefore, dispense with attending to the king's message. Accordingly, the question is reduced to this point, not whether the king could arm, for of that there is no doubt, but whether the supplies demanded, be necessary, a matter as little doubtful. I give it as my opinion, that the message of the king be taken into immediate consideration."

After long debates, the form of a decree presented by Mirabeau, was adopted in the following terms:

" The National Assembly decrees, that its president shall, in the course of the day, attend the king, for the purpose of thanking his majesty, for the measures which he hath taken for the preservation of peace. The Assembly decrees, moreover, that, on to-morrow the 16th of May,

the

the order of the day ſhall be the following queſtion relative to the conſtitution: *Ought the nation to entruſt the king with the exerciſe of the right of making war and peace?"*

MAY 20, 1790.

Firſt Speech on the right of making War and Peace.

From the 16th, the grand queſtion ſtated in the decree of the 15th, was the ſubject of the moſt brilliant debates.

A great number of orators had now been heard. Some were for attributing to the king excluſively, the right of making war and peace. Others claimed likewiſe the excluſive exerciſe of that right, for the legiſlative body.

MIRABEAU.

"In rising to speak upon a subject, which, for these five days past, hath occasioned such long debates, my sole motive is to rectify* the state of the question, which, in my mind, hath not been fixed where it should have been. Urgent peril at the present moment, dangers of no common magnitude in future, ought to have roused all the attention of patriotism: but this important question is likewise accompanied, with a danger peculiar to itself. These words, war and peace, sound loftily to the ear, awake and deceive the imagination, inflame the most imperious of the passions, pride and courage, are connected with the grandest objects, victories, conquests, the fate of empires, above all, with liberty, with the

* Etablir.

duration

duration of that infant conſtitution, which every Frenchman hath ſworn to maintain: and when a queſtion of public right, preſents itſelf with ſo impoſing an aſpect, what attention ſhould not one pay to oneſelf, in order to reconcile, in ſo ſolemn a diſcuſſion, the cool reaſon, the profound meditation of the ſtateſman, with that emotion, ſo excuſable, which the fears that ſurround us muſt inſpire?

"Are we to delegate to the king, the exerciſe of the right of making war and peace, or ought we to attribute it to the legiſlative body? It is thus, gentlemen, it is with this alternative, that hitherto the queſtion hath been ſtated; and I confeſs that this manner of ſtating it, would render it a queſtion not to be ſolved by me. I do not think that we can, without annihilating the conſtitution, entruſt the king with the exerciſe,

exercise, of the right of making peace or war; as little do I think, that we can exclusively adjudge this right to the legislative body, without preparing for ourselves dangers of another kind, and equally to be dreaded. But are we under an obligation to make an exclusive choice? Can we not, in favour of one of the functions of the government, at once partaking both of action and of will, of execution and of deliberation, make the two powers, which constitute the national strength, and have been sanctioned by our constitution?

" Before we come to any decision upon this new point of view, I must first examine, in concert with you, gentlemen, whether, in the practice of war and peace, the nature of things, their irresistible progress point not out to us the junctures, when each of the two powers may act separately,

separately, the points of contact where their co-operation commences, the functions which are common to them, and those which are peculiar, the moment for deliberation, and the moment which calls for action. Be assured, gentlemen, that such an inquiry will conduct us much more readily to the truth, than if we were to confine ourselves to simple theory.

" And first, is it for the king or for the legislative body, to maintain foreign connections, to watch over the safety of the empire, to make, to order the preparations necessary for its defence?

" Should you determine this first question in favour of the king, and I know not how you can determine it otherwise, without creating in the same kingdom two executive powers, you are by that alone obliged to acknowledge, that, frequently,

frequently, a firſt act of hoſtility ſhall be repulſed, before the legiſlative body hath had time to manifeſt any ſymptoms, either of approbation, or of diſapprobation. Now, what is ſuch act of hoſtility committed and repulſed, but a ſtate of war, if not in will, at leaſt in fact?

"I pauſe at this firſt hypotheſis, in order to make you ſenſible of its truth and of its conſequences. A ſquadron is ſent out for the protection of our colonies; troops are ſtationed upon our frontiers. You admit that theſe preparations, that theſe means of defence, appertain to the royal authority. Now, if that ſquadron be attacked, if thoſe troops be threatened, will they, ere they defend themſelves, wait till the legiſlative body ſhall have approved or diſapproved the war? No, undoubtedly. I conclude, from that ſingle circumſtance,

circumstance, that war exists, and that the signal for it hath been given by necessity. Hence it arises, that, in almost every case, there can be no room for deliberation, unless in order to determine, whether a first act of hostility shall be followed up with consequences, that is, whether the state of war should be continued. I say, in almost every case; in fact, gentlemen, it will never become a question with the French, whose constitution hath so lately refined their ideas of justice, to make or to concert an offensive war, that is, to attack the neighbouring states, when those states give us no cause to complain of them. Upon this supposition, undoubtedly, deliberation should take the lead of preparation; but such a war ought to be considered as a crime, and I intend to make it a subject of an article of decree.

" The

"The point, then, under discussion, relates only to a defensive war, where the enemy hath committed hostilities; and here we find ourselves in a passive state of war: or where, without hostilities having been as yet commenced, the preparations of the enemy give notice of the intention; and in that case, the peace being, by that single circumstance, disturbed, preparations of defence become, on our part, indispensable.

"There is a third case; which is, when it is necessary to determine, whether a right contested or usurped shall be resumed, or asserted by force of arms; and I shall not forget to enlarge upon it; but, until then, I do not see that there can be any occasion for the legislative body to deliberate. The time will come, when the preparations for defence, exceeding the ordinary

ordinary estimates, the necessity for making still greater preparations must be notified to the legislative body, and it is my purpose to state to you what are its rights in that case.

" But how! you will say, shall not the legislative body be at all times possessed, of the power of preventing the commencement of the state of war? No; for that would be like asking, whether there be any method of preventing a neighbouring nation from attacking us; and what method should you take?

" Would you make no preparations? you will not repel hostilities, but endure them. The state of war will remain the same.

" Will you charge the legislative body with the care of making defensive preparations? you will not thereby prevent the attack; and how would you reconcile such action of the legislative body, with that of the executive power?

"Will you compel the executive power, to notify to you its most inconsiderable preparations, its most unimportant measures? you will, by so doing, violate every rule of prudence; the enemy, acquainted with all your precautions, all your measures, will make sport of them; you will render preparations nugatory: it were better not to order them.

"Will you limit the extent of the preparations? But can you do so, with respect to all the points of contact, which connect you with Europe, India, America, the whole globe? But must not your preparations be proportioned to those made by the neighbouring states? But may not hostilities as well commence,

between

between two ships as between two squadrons? But will you not be obliged to grant, every year, a certain sum, for unexpected armaments? Must not that sum be according to the extent of your coasts, to the importance of your commerce, to the distance of your transmarine possessions, to the strength exerted by your enemies? Nevertheless, gentlemen, I feel as forcibly as any one, how necessary it is to take care, that our vigilance be not surprised by such difficulties: for it is of moment, that there should exist some check upon the executive power, to prevent it from abusing even the right of watching over our security; from wasting immense sums in useless armaments; from levying forces for itself, under pretence of leading them against an enemy; from exciting, by too great an apparatus of defence,

fence, the jealousy or the fear of our neighbours. Undoubtedly, we must guard against these evils; but the natural course of events shews us, how the legislative body may repress abuses of this kind; for, on the one hand, should there be a necessity for armaments more considerable, than the war-extraordinaries are equal to, the executive power may not undertake them, without being duly authorized; and the right will remain with you, of insisting upon a negotiation of peace, of refusing the supplies demanded. On the other hand, will not the immediate notification, which the executive power shall be obliged to make, respecting the state of war, whether impending or commenced, leave you all the means imaginable of watching over public liberty?

" Here, gentlemen, I take in the third case

case of which I have spoken, that of a war to be undertaken, for the recovery or the conservation of a possession or a right; a case which belongs to the description of war definitive. It seems at first view, that, in such an hypothesis, the legislative body would have to deliberate, even with respect to the preparations; but endeavour to apply this case, endeavour to realize this hypothesis. Is any right usurped or contested? The executive power, charged with what relates to foreign connections, attempts, at first, to recover the right by negotiation. Should this first step prove unsuccessful, and the right be of importance, still leave to the executive power the right of preparing for defence; oblige it to notify to the representatives of the nation, the usurpation complained of, the right which is claimed, in the same manner as it shall be obliged to notify a war impending or commenced. You will by these means establish a uniform course of procedure, in every case; and I am now going to demonstrate, that it is sufficient that the co-operation of the legislative power commence, at the time of the notification of which I have just spoken, in order perfectly to reconcile the interest of the nation, with the maintenance of the public force.

" Hostilities, then, are either commenced or impending. In that case, what are the duties of the executive power? What are the rights of the legislative?

" I have just been declaring them; the executive power is to notify, without delay, the state of the war, either as existing, or as approaching, or as necessary; to make known its causes, to ask for supplies,

plies, to re-assemble the legislative body, if it be not already assembled.

"The legislative body, in its turn, hath four sorts of measures to take. The first is, to inquire whether, hostilities being commenced, our ministers, or some agent of the executive power, have not been the culpable aggressors. In such a case, the author of the aggression should be impeached as guilty of high treason against the nation. Make such a law, and you will confine your wars to the sole exercise of the right of just defence; and you will have done more for public liberty, than if, in order to attribute the exclusive right of war to the representative body, you should lose the advantages derivable from royalty.

"The second measure is, to approve, to determine upon the war, if it be necessary, to disapprove it, if it be useless or unjust; to require the king to set on foot a negotiation for peace, and to compel him to that measure, by refusing the supplies; and in this, gentlemen, consists the true right of the legislative body. Here the powers are not confounded; the forms of the different branches of the government are not violated, and the national interest is preserved. But further, gentlemen; when I propose the approbation or disapprobation of the war, by the legislative body, while I refuse it the exclusive right of deliberating on war and peace, do not imagine that, by so doing, I am eluding the question, or exhibiting the same subject of debate in a different form. The exercise of the right of making peace and war, is neither simply an action, nor yet merely an operation of the will; on the

the contrary, it is connected with both these principles: it requires the concurrence of the two powers; and the whole theory of this question consists only in assigning, to the legislative body and to the executive power respectively, the kind of co-operation which, from its nature, is most proper for it. To give the legislative body the exclusive deliberation upon peace and war, a right which, in ancient times, was enjoyed by the Roman senate, a right enjoyed, in modern days, by the states of Sweden, by the diet of Poland, by the confederation of Holland, were transforming the king of France into a stadtholder, or a consul; it were selecting from the two delegates of the nation, that delegate which, however unceasingly purified by the choice of the people, by the continual renovation of the elections,

elections, nevertheless cannot solely and exclusively deliberate, with any degree of usefulness, upon an occasion of that nature. On the contrary, to confer upon the legislative power the right of deliberating in the shape of approbation, disapprobation, requisition of peace, prosecution of a guilty minister, refusal of supplies, is allowing it to co-operate in the exercise of a national right, by the means which are suited to the nature of such a body.

" This difference, then, is very remarkable, and leads to the desired end, by preserving the two powers in their entire perfection; whereas, otherwise, you would lie under the pernicious necessity of making an exclusive choice, between two delegates which ought to proceed hand in hand.

" The third measure of the legislative body,

body, confifts in a continuation of the means which I point out, and the right of which means I affign to it.

" The firft of thefe means is, to admit of no recefs, as long as the war continues.

" The fecond, to prolong the feffion, in the cafe of an impending war.

" The third, to affemble the national guard of the kingdom, in fuch numbers as fhall be deemed neceffary, whenever the king fhall carry on a war in perfon.

" The fourth (even after having approved the war), to require, as often as it fhall be deemed expedient, the executive power to negotiate a peace.

" I paufe for a moment upon the two means laft mentioned, as they difplay in perfection the fyftem which I propofe.

" On account of the poffible danger, in

in appropriating the deliberations on war directly and exclusively to the legislative body, some maintain that the right of war and peace appertains to the monarch alone; they affect even to doubt, that the nation can lawfully dispose of this right, although she hath had the power of delegating the sovereignty. What? is it, indeed, a matter of no importance in their eyes, to place beside the constitution an unlimited authority, always able to overturn it? Do they wish to cherish this constitution? Would they render it immortal, like justice and reason?

" On the other hand, because the co-operation of the monarch, in exercising the right of making peace and war, may be attended with danger (and, in fact, it is the case), others give it as their opinion, that we ought to deprive him of even the right

right of co-operation. Now, are they not, in this, defiring an impoffibility, unlefs you take away from the king the preparations for peace and war? Are they not defiring what is unconftitutional, fince your decrees have allowed the king a fort of co-operation, even in acts which are purely legiflative? For my part, I am eftablifhing the counterpoife of the dangers, which may arife from the royal power, in the conftitution itfelf, in the balancing both powers, in the concurrence of the two delegates of the nation, in the internal force which you will derive from that national guard (the only counterpoife fuited to a reprefentative government), againft an army ftationed on the frontiers. Congratulate yourfelves, gentlemen, on this difcovery. If your conftitution be unfhakeable, it is to fuch an equilibrium

that

that you will be indebted for its stability.

"Again: in conferring upon the legislative body, even after it hath approved the war, the right of requiring the executive power to negotiate a peace, take notice, that I do not mean to give exclusively to the legislative body, the right of deliberating on peace; for that were to relapse into all the inconveniences, of which I have already made mention. Who shall know the critical moment to think of making peace, if it be not he who holds the thread of all political relations? Will you determine, likewise, that the agents employed for that purpose shall correspond with none but you? Are you to issue instructions to them? Are you to answer their dispatches? Are you to dismiss them, and appoint others in their room, should they

they fail to fulfil your expectations? Will you disclose, in the course of solemn debates, demanded by some member of the legislative body, the secret motives by which you are actuated in your endeavours to make peace, which would frequently prove the most certain method of not obtaining it? and, even when our enemies shall desire peace as much as we, is your loyalty to impose a law on you prohibiting all concealment; and will you likewise force the envoys of the powers then at variance with you, to the noise and notoriety of a public debate*?

" I distinguish, then, the right of requiring the executive power to make peace, from an order issued for its conclusion, and from the exclusive exercise of the right of making peace; for is there any other mode of acting up to the

* A l'éclat d'une discussion.

national intereſt, than that which I am propoſing? When war is commenced, it is no longer in the power of a nation to make peace; will even the order for withdrawing the troops arreſt the progreſs of the enemy? Should one be diſpoſed to make ſome ſacrifices, can one tell whether the conditions will not prove ſo oppreſſive, that honour muſt forbid their being accepted? Nay, ſuppoſing the negotiations for a peace already opened, will a ceſſation of the war enſue, as the neceſſary and immediate conſequence? It is, then, the province of the executive power, to chooſe the proper juncture for entering upon negotiation, to prepare for it in ſilence, to conduct it with ability: it is the province of the legiſlative power to beſeech the executive, to attend without intermiſſion to that momentous object;

it

it is for the legislative power to punish the guilty minister or agent, who, invested with such a function, should neglect to fulfil its duties; it is also for the legislative to ratify the treaty, as soon as the articles are agreed upon. These, gentlemen, are the limits which the interest of the public does not suffer us to transgress, and which the very nature of things hath marked out for us.

" In fine, the fourth measure of the legislative body, is, to redouble its attention, in order to reduce, incontinently, the public force to its permanent footing, as soon as the war is at an end. Issue orders for disbanding incontinently the regiments extraordinary, appoint a short day for their separation, limit the continuation of their pay to that term; render the minister responsible; pursue him as a criminal,

criminal, if orders so important be left unexecuted: this too is what the interest of the public prescribes to you.

"I have followed, gentlemen, the same line of questions, in inquiring to whom ought to belong the right of forming treaties of alliance, of commerce, and all those other conventions which may be necessary to the well-being of the state. I first asked myself, whether we ought to renounce making treaties; and this question is reduced to the inquiry, whether, in the actual state of our commerce and that of Europe, we should leave to chance the influence of the other powers over us, and our re-action upon Europe; whether, because we shall on a sudden change our political system (and indeed, how many errors, how many prejudices shall we not have to overturn!), we shall oblige

oblige other nations to change theirs; whether, for any long time, our peace and that of the other powers of Europe can be otherwife preferved, than by a balance which forbids the fudden confederacy, of feveral nations againſt one? The time will come, undoubtedly, when we fhall have friends only, and not allies, when liberty of commerce will be univerfal, when Europe will be only one great family; but hope too hath her enthufiafm; fhall we be fo fortunate as to find, that the miracle to which we are indebted for our freedom, fhould, at the felf-fame inſtant, be brilliantly repeated in both hemifpheres*?

"If, however, treaties we muſt have, he alone may prepare them, conclude them, who fhall poſſefs the right of negotiation:

---

* Se répète avec éclat dans les deux mondes?

tiation: for I do not see how it can be either useful, or conformable to the foundations of our government already consecrated, to enact, that the legislative body shall communicate with foreign powers, without any intervening agent. Those treaties will be notified to you immediately; those treaties will be in force, only so far as the legislative body shall have approved them. Here again, then, you have before you the just limits of that concurrence, between the two powers, the executive and the legislative. Nor will it even be sufficient, to refuse your approbation to a treaty of a dangerous tendency; the responsibility of ministers presents you with the means, of likewise punishing the guilty author of that treaty.

" I am not inquiring, whether it were more advantageous, that a treaty should not

not be concluded, until after it hath been approved of by the legiſlative body: for, is it not evident that the reſult is the ſame, and that it is much more advantageous to ourſelves, that a treaty ſhould become irrevocable, on the ſole account that it ſhall have been ratified by the legiſlative body, than that, even after approbation given, the other powers ſhould ſtill be at liberty to reject it?

" And are there not ſome other precautions to be taken with regard to treaties; and were it not becoming the dignity, the loyalty of a national convention, to determine beforehand, for this and for all other nations, not what treaties may be permitted to compriſe, but what they never ſhall compriſe in any reſpect whatever? My thoughts upon this point coincide with the opinion of ſeveral who

have

have already spoken; I am for having it declared, that the French nation renounces conquest of every shape and kind, and that it never will employ its force against the liberty of any people.

" Such, gentlemen, is the system which I have formed in my own mind, respecting the exercise of the right of war and peace. But I must offer some additional motives for my opinion; I ought, especially, to make known, why I am so forcibly attached, to the idea of giving the legislative body, only a co-operation necessary to the exercise of that right, instead of assigning it to that body exclusively. The co-operation which I have mentioned, can alone prevent all those dangers.

" And, in the first place, to shew you that I have not shut my eyes against any objection,

objection, the following is my creed, as to the theory of the question, considered independantly of its political relations. Undoubtedly, peace and war are acts of sovereignty, belonging to the nation alone. Can this principle be denied, unless we take for granted that nations are slaves? But the question does not turn upon the right itself, the question is concerning the delegation.

" Again: although all the preparations, and the whole direction of war and peace, appertain to the action of the executive power, it cannot be denied that the declaring war and peace, is an act of pure will; that every act of hostility, every treaty of peace, may be, in some measure, thus interpreted: *I, the nation, make war, I, the nation, make peace*; consequently, how can one man alone, how can a king, a minifter, become the organ of the general will? How can the executor of that general will be at the fame time its organ?

"Equally am I aware of all the dangers which can arife, from entrufting a fingle perfon with the right, or rather with the means of ruining the ftate, of difpofing of the citizens, of rifking the fafety of the empire, of bringing down upon our heads, like fome mifchievous imp of darknefs, every fcourge which is the companion of war. And here, like fo many others, have I fummoned to my recollection, the names of thofe wicked minifters, who kindled accurfed wars, either to render themfelves neceffary, or to keep a rival at a diftance. Here have I beheld all Europe in a flame, only becaufe the glove of a duchefs was not picked up the very moment fhe dropped it, it *. I reprefent to my imagination this warrior-king and conqueror, attaching to himfelf the foldiery by corruption and fuccefs, tempted to re-become † a defpot, on arriving in his own territory, cherifhing a party within the empire, and overturning the conftitution with that very hand, which had been armed by the conftitution, and by the conftitution only.

"Well, gentlemen, let us confider of thefe objections, let us enquire, whether the means propofed for warding off thefe dangers, will not pave the way for other dangers not lefs formidable, not lefs fatal to public liberty.

"I have but one word to fay, as to the principles. Undoubtedly, the king is not the organ of the public will, but neither

---

* Pour le gand d'une ducheffe trop tard ramaffé.
† Redevenir.

is he a stranger to the declaration of that will. Accordingly, in confining myself to require the co-operation of the two delegates of the nation, I am perfectly acting up to constitutional principles.

"Again : I wish you to take notice, that, in inquiring whether the right of sovereignty, should be appropriated to this or that delegate of the nation, in preference to the other, to the delegate called *the king*, or to the delegate gradually purified and renewed, which is named *the legislative body*, we must banish all trite notions of any delegate being superior to controul[*]; that it is the privilege of the nation to prefer which delegate she pleases, for the execution of such individual act of her will; that the sole question therefore is,

[*] Incomptabilité.

since we determine the choice, to confult, not the national pride, but the public intereft, the only ambition that fhould infpire a great people, and the only one that is worthy of it *. All fubtilty therefore difappears, in order to make room for this queftion :

" By whom is it moft ufeful that the right of making peace or war fhould be exercifed ?

" Obferve, moreover, that this point of view is a ftranger to my fyftem; it is for thofe to anfwer the objection of unaccountability †, who are inclined to attribute

---

* Seule et digne ambition d'un grand peuple.

† Incomptabilité.

Copious as our language is, we are not fufficiently furnifhed with thofe polyfyllables, which exprefs in one word what, otherwife, muft be expreffed by

tribute exclufively to the king, the exercife of the right of making war and peace; but I combat this fyftem, in concert with all good citizens. An exclufive right is talked of; and I am talking of only co-operation.

"The danger of each fyftem is now difplayed before our eyes.

"I put the queftion to yourfelves: fhall we be better affured of having none but juft and equitable wars, if the exercife of the right of making war, be exclufively delegated to an affembly of feven hundred perfons? Have you foerfeen

---

by a periphrafe. We want a fupply of thofe *alities*, *ilities*, *abilities* and *ifibilities*, with which the French feem to have ftocked themfelves in modern days. For inftance, we have no fuch word as *annuality*; its true Englifh drefs were *yearlinefs*; but have we any fuch word as *yearlinefs*? W.

how

how far excited paffions, to what lengths towering courage and miftaken dignity, may carry, and even juftify, imprudence? We have heard one of our orators propofe to you, fhould England unjuftly attack Spain, to crofs the feas incontinently, to whelm one nation upon the other, to play out the game to the laft livre, to the laft man, with thofe imperious Englifh, in the very heart of London,—and we all applauded what he faid; I caught myfelf in the fact of applauding him; and a tranfport, the refult of eloquence*, fufficed to impofe, for a moment, upon your wifdom. Do you imagine that fuch tranfports, fhould the legiflative body ever deliberate directly and exclufively, will not hurry you into wars fraught with infinite difafters, and that you will never

---

* Un mouvement oratoire.

confound the counsels of courage with the counsels of experience? While one of your members is proposing deliberation, his voice will be drowned in the clamour for a war*; you will see yourselves surrounded by battalions of armed citizens. You are not likely to be deceived by ministers; shall you never be deceived by yourselves?

"There is yet a danger of another kind, which is peculiar to the legislative body, when exercising exclusively the right of peace and war; and that is, that such a body cannot be subjected to any sort of responsibility. I am well aware that a victim, is a feeble satisfaction for the crimes of an unjust war; but, when talking of responsibility, I am not talking of revenge. This minister, who you sup-

* On demandera la guerre à grands cris.

pose is to conduct himself according to caprice alone, must expect to be brought to trial, his head shall be the price of his imprudence. You have had more than one Louvois under the fostering care of despotism; are you to have a second brood of them, under the auspices of liberty?

"Some talk of public opinion, as a restraint upon the representatives of the nation; but public opinion, frequently led astray, even by sentiments worthy of panegyric, will serve only to seduce you; but public opinion does not separately influence each member of a great assembly.

"That Roman, who, bearing war in the folds of his gown, threatened, while he unrolled them, to scatter every scourge of war upon the enemy, must have felt the full importance of his mission. He stood alone; a mighty destiny was in his hands;

he was the messenger of terror; but had the crowded senate, which, in the midst of a stormy and impassioned debate, dispatched him on that embassy, experienced that fear, which the doubtful, the dreadful issue * of the war should have inspired? You have been already desired, gentlemen, to cast your eyes upon free states; it was by wars the most ambitious, the most barbarous, that they were perpetually distinguished.

" Cast your eyes on political assemblies; it hath always been under the magic influence of passion, that they have decreed war. You are all acquainted with the anecdote of the sailor, who, in the year 1740, determined England to resolve

---

* Le redoubtable et douteux avenir.—Here a slight transposition improves the sentence; for, in the original, there is a species of *bathos*.

upon a war with Spain. *When the Spaniards, after mutilating me, were for putting me to death, I commended my soul to God, and my vengeance to my country.* The sailor was a true orator; but the war which he kindled was neither politic nor just; neither the king, nor the ministry of England were inclined to it. The emotions of an assembly, though less numerous, and more liable than ours to the combinations of insidious policy*, decided in that affair.

" Attend now to still more important considerations. Are not you apprehensive, gentlemen, of the internal dissensions, which an unexpected debate on war, war

---

* Can there be a better argument than this, in favour of the plan, proposed by one of our own orators lately deceased, for increasing the number of representatives in the House of Commons ? W.

undertaken without the king's concurrence, by the legiflative body, might give birth to, not only within its own walls, but likewife throughout the kingdom? Frequently, where two parties fhall violently embrace oppofite opinions, the deliberation will be the fruit of an obftinate ftruggle, decided merely by a few fuffrages; and, in fuch a cafe, fhould the fame fpirit of divifion take poffeffion of the public mind, what fuccefs are you to hope for, from a war which a great part of the nation difapproves? Obferve the diet of Poland: not feldom a debate on war only begets a civil war amongft themfelves. Turn your view to what hath juft paffed in Sweden. In vain hath the king contrived to extort the fuffrages of the ftates; the diffidents have nearly gained the guilty fuccefs of rendering

the

the war abortive*. Already had Holland prefented the fame fpectacle. War was declared againft the wifh of a fimple ftadtholder: what fruit have we reaped from an alliance which had coft us fo much care, fo much treafure? We are going, then, to fow the feeds of civil diffenfions in our conftitution, if we confer on the legiflative body the exclufive exercife of the right of war; and, as the *veto* fufpenfive, which you have granted to the king, could not in any wife be applied to fuch deliberations, the diffenfions of which I fpeak will prove only the more formidable.

" I paufe, gentlemen, for an inftant, upon the reflection juft made, in order to give you to underftand, that, in the practice of governments, one is often obliged

* De faire échouer la guerre.

to depart, and that too for the public interest, from the rigid purity of philosophical abstraction. You yourselves have decreed, that the executor of the national will should, in certain cases, enjoy the right of suspending, the effect of the first manifestation of that national will; that he might appeal from the known will of the representatives of the nation, to the presumed will of the nation itself. Now, if we have given such a concurrence to the monarch, even in legislative acts, which are so foreign to the action of the executive power, how, if we follow the chain of the same principles, can we avoid making the king co-operate, I do not say merely in the direction of the war, but in the deliberation on the war?

"Let us ward off, if we ought, the danger of civil dissensions. Will you as easily

easily avoid the danger, resulting from the slowness of deliberations on such a subject, unless you confine the object to those cases only, where the concurrence, or the will of the legislative body, is become indispensable? Are you not apprehensive, that your public force may be palsied, as is actually the case in Poland, in Holland, and in every republic? Are you not apprehensive, that this slowness may yet increase, either because our constitution is insensibly taking the form of a grand confederation, or because the departments must unavoidably acquire, a vast influence over the legislative body? Are you not apprehensive, that the people, hearing that its representatives are making a direct declaration of war in its name, may not thereby receive a dangerous impulse towards democracy, or, what is still worse, towards oligarchy; that the inclination for war or peace may originate in the very provinces, be soon after displayed in petitions, and impart to a mighty mass of men, that agitation which so important an object is capable of exciting? Are you not apprehensive, that the legislative body, notwithstanding its wisdom, may be driven to overleap the boundaries of its powers, by the almost inevitable consequences attending the exclusive exercise of the right of war and peace? Are you not apprehensive, that, in order to second the succesful efforts of a war, which it shall have voted without the co-operation of the monarch, it may be desirous of influencing the direction of that war, the choice of generals, particularly where any ill success can be imputed to them; and that this restless vigilance,

gilance, which, in fact, were a second executive power, may encroach upon the province of the supreme head of the nation?

"Again: do you count as nothing, the inconvenience of an assembly not permanent, obliged to re-assemble at the time which should be employed in deliberation; the uncertainty, the hesitation which will accompany every step taken by the executive power, which will never know how far the provisional orders may extend; the inconveniences of even a public and unexpected debate, upon the motives for making preparations for war or peace; a debate, of which all the secrets of state (and such secrets we shall have for a long time to come) often form the elementary matter?

"In fine, do you esteem as nothing, the danger

danger of introducing republican forms, into a government which is at once representative and monarchical? I beseech you to consider this danger, with reference to the constitution, to ourselves, and to the king.

"With respect to the constitution, can we hope to preserve it, if we compose our government of different forms, at variance with one another? I myself have maintained, that there exists but one sole principle of government for all nations, I mean their own sovereignty; but it is not less certain, that the different modes of delegating the powers, bestow on the governments of different nations different forms, the union, the *tout ensemble*, of which constitute their whole force, and the opposition of which, on the other hand, gives birth to an eternal spirit of discord in a

state,

state, until the form which predominates have overturned all the rest; and thence arise, independently of despotism, those convulsions which prove the downfal of empires.

"Rome owed her destruction to this mixture of royalty, aristocracy*, and democracy. The tempests which have often agitated several states of Europe, were de-

---

* With all due deference to this great statesman, it was to the want of such a mixture, that Rome owed the loss of her liberty. *Cicero*, and that profound politician *Tacitus*, were decidedly of opinion, that the just mixture of the three powers of monarchy, aristocracy, and democracy, was the sublimity of human government, but looked upon it as a delicious picture of the imagination, which they rather wished, than expected to see realized. But without resorting to antiquity, our own admirable and enviable constitution is a sufficient proof of the excellence of the three powers, mixt and balanced. Perhaps the French may yet repent the utter expulsion of aristocracy. W.

rived

rived from no other origin. Men adhere to the diſtribution of the powers; the powers are exerciſed by men; men, abuſing an authority not ſufficiently reſtrained, overleap its boundaries. Thus it is that monarchy exalts itſelf into deſpotiſm: and here you have a reaſon why we ſhould take ſo many precautions. But thus it is, alſo, that repreſentative government degenerates into oligarchy, whenever two powers, intended to counterpoiſe each other, make encroachments, and mutually invade, inſtead of mutually reſtraining.

"Now, gentlemen, excepting the ſingle caſe of a republic properly ſo called, or of a grand confederation unprovided with a ſole chief, or a monarchy where the chief is reduced to a ſplendid cypher*, quote me an inſtance of any nation, which hath aſſigned the exerciſe of the right of war

---

* A une vaine repréſentation.

and

and peace, exclusively to a senate. It may be proved very well, in theory, that the executive power shall preserve its full force, if all the preparations, all the direction, all the action belong to the king, and if the legislative body have only the exclusive right of saying, *I will have war, or I will have peace.* But shew me how the representative body, pressing so closely on the executive power, can avoid overstepping the almost imperceptible limits which occasion their separation. I am sensible that the separation still exists. Action is not will; but this line of demarkation* is much more easily demonstrated than preserved; and is it not

---

* Strange, that we have no such word as this in *Johnson's* dictionary! Surely it is time to review our language, and, in place of that crowd of obsolete and useless invalids, introduce stout recruits, though enlisted in foreign countries. W.

running the hazard of confounding the two powers, or rather is it not confounding them already, in the real practice of civil polity, to suffer them to approach so nearly to each other? Besides, is it not departing from those principles, which already have been sanctioned by the constitution?

"If I examine the inconveniences, resulting from the exclusive right given to the legislative body, as far as it respects ourselves, that is, with respect to the obstacles, which the enemies of the public good have opposed unceasingly to your career, what a multitude of new adversaries are you not going to stir up, amongst those who have hoped to reconcile all the energy of liberty, with the exercise of the royal prerogative? I am speaking of those only, not of the flatterers, not of the courtiers, not of those
de enerate

degenerate beings who prefer defpotifm to liberty; not of thofe who, in this tribune, have had the affurance to maintain, that we had no right to alter the conftitution, or that the exercife of the right of peace and war, is infeparable from royalty, or that the council fo often corrupted, which, like fatellites, furrounds kings, conveys with more fidelity the public fenfe of intereft, than reprefentatives elected by the people. It is not of fuch blafphemers, nor of their impious tenets, nor of their impotent attempts, that I am inclined to make mention, but of thofe men, who, formed for liberty, are in dread, neverthelefs, of the commotions incident to popular ftates, of thofe men, who, after having confidered the permanence of a national affembly, as the fole barrier againft defpotifm, confider alfo the royal power as a useful barrier against aristocracy*.

* After all, this question of *aristocracy* is a difficult one for France. I have read no publications upon the late revolution, excepting Mr. *Burke's* invective. But all sober spectators, reflecting on our own government, seem to wish for a just mixture of aristocracy in the new French constitution. But the nobles of France compose a multitude; the nobility of England is but a handful. To admit *all* the nobles of France to an hereditary share in the legislature, might, if they threw their weight into the scale of royalty, prove of dangerous consequence to the democratic interest. Who can say that they would not look for the resurrection of their deceased privileges? Again: admit but *a part* of them; who shall be received, who excluded? an inexhaustible source of discord. Again: instead of granting them hereditary seats, decree that the upper house shall be elective; another source of discord. What violence, what venality, what crimes of every hue, would not accompany such elections? Perhaps, all that one can well say to the French in this knotty business is, *God guide ye.* W.

" In

" In fine, with reference to the king, with reference to his succeſſors, what will be the inevitable effect of a law, which concentred exclusively in the legiſlative body, the right of making peace or war? To weak kings, the privation of authority will prove only a cauſe of diſcouragement and inactivity; but is the royal dignity, then, no longer to make a part of the nation's property? A king encompaſſed with perfidious counsellors, perceiving himſelf to be no longer on an equality with other kings, will imagine himſelf dethroned; he might be inſenſible of his loſs, until perſuaded of it by others; and things owe all their value, and, to a certain degree, their reality, to opinion alone. An upright monarch will believe, that, at leaſt, the throne is environed by quickſands and all the ſprings of the public force will loſe

lose their elasticity *. An ambitious prince, discontented with the lot which the constitution hath assigned to him, will become the enemy of that constitution, of which he ought to be the guarantee and guardian.

"Must we, then, on this account, return to our late slavery? must we, in order to lessen the number of the malcontents, stain our immortal constitution by the adoption of false measures, by the adoption of false principles? This is not what I propose, since, on the contrary, the question is, whether the double co-operation which I allow to the two powers, the executive and legislative, in the exercise of the right of peace and war, were not more favourable to national liberty.

* Se relâcheront.

" Imagine

"Imagine not that I have been seduced by the example of England, who leaves to her king the entire exercife of the right of making war and peace. I myfelf condemn this example.

"In England, the king is not confined to the repulfing hoftilities; he commences them, he orders them; and I, on the contrary, propofe to you to profecute as criminals, the minifters, or their agents, who fhall have made offenfive war.

"In England, the monarch declares war by a fimple proclamation in his own name; and fuch a proclamation being an undoubted national act, I am very far from thinking, either that it fhould be made in the king's name, in a free nation, or that there can be a declaration of war, without the concurrence of the legiflative body.

" In England, the king is not obliged to convoke the parliament, at the commencement of a war; and frequently, during a long interval, the legiflative body unaffembled, is deprived of all means of influence; while the monarch, difplaying all the forces of the empire, embarks the nation in meafures, which fhe will be incapable of preventing, when, at length, fhe is confulted*. On the contrary, I

propofe

---

* Here I believe all admirers of our excellent conftitution will differ from M. *Mirabeau*. As long as parliament holds the ftrings of the purfe, the king, indeed, may commence a war, but I defy him to carry it on. And even, fhould a war be entered upon, during the interval between one feffion and another, the right of impeachment at a future day, is an awful check upon adminiftration. If an Englifh minifter hath any regard for his place, or for his head, he will be careful of going to war,

without

propose to oblige the king to notify, incontinently, the hostilities either impending or commenced, and to decree that the legislative body shall be then instantly re-assembled.

"In England, the head of the state can make war for his own aggrandizement, for the sake of conquest, that is, in order to exercise the trade of tyranny. On the contrary, I propose to you to declare to all Europe, that you will never employ

without first founding the inclination of the public. The stern disapprobation of the people's representatives, either at or after the commencement of a war, is what no wise minister will risk incurring, and what, if he were to risk it, he could not withstand. Doubtless, few of my readers are unacquainted with M. *De Lolme's* ingenious book upon the English Constitution: he hath there treated of the point above-mentioned, in a manner that might have satisfied even M. de *Mirabeau*. W.

the public force against the liberty of any nation.

"In England, the king experiences no other obstacle, than the refusal of parliamentary supplies; and the enormous debt of the nation is an ample proof, that that barrier is insufficient, and that the art of impoverishing nations is an engine of despotism, equally formidable with any other. On the contrary, I propose to you to appropriate to the legislative body, the right of approving or disapproving the war, of preventing any recourse being had to force of arms, when there hath not yet been any hostility; and the right, even after the war hath met with approbation, of requesting the monarch to negotiate a peace.

"In fine, the militia of England is not organized in such a manner, as to counterpoise terpoife the public force, which is entirely in the hands of the fovereign. Now, I propofe, on the contrary, that, in cafe the king makes war in perfon, the legiflative body fhall be invefted with the right, of affembling fuch a portion of the national guard, and in fuch place, as it fhall deem expedient. And, undoubtedly, fhould this precaution appear dangerous or ufelefs, you will at leaft organize that internal force in fuch a manner, as to form an army for the defence of public liberty, as you have already raifed one for the protection of your frontiers.

"Let us now fee whether there ftill remain any objections, which I have not overturned in the fyftem which I oppofe.

"The king, then, it is faid, will be able to carry on unjuft wars, wars which are anti-national! But fuch an objection, gentlemen, cannot be pointed againft me, who am for granting to the king only a simple co-operation, in the exercise of the right of war; and I would fain know from yourselves, how anti-national wars could have any place in my system. Can you, really and truly, deny the influence of a legislative body, continually present, continually on the watch; which will have it in its power not only to refuse supplies, but also to approve or disapprove the war, but also to request a negotiation of peace? Nay more, do you account as nothing, the influence of a nation organized in every part, and which is perpetually to exercise the right of petitioning according to legal forms ? A despotic monarch might be arrested in his progress; and shall not a citizen-king, a king placed in the midst of an armed people, be subject to the like controul ?

" It is asked, who is to watch over the kin dom,

kingdom, when the executive power shall put in motion all its force? I answer, the law, the constitution, the equilibrium ever maintained between the force internal and the force external.

"It is said, that *we are not cut out* for liberty, like the English*; but we are possessed of greater means for the preservation of liberty, and therefore I propose greater precautions.

"Our constitution is not yet established; a war may be lighted up, with no other view than to gain a pretext for calling out a mighty force, and for soon turning that force against us. Well, let us pay a proper attention to such fears; but let us distinguish the present moment from the durable effects of a constitution, and let us not consider as everlasting, the provisional

* Encadrés.

dispositions,

dispositions, which the extraordinary circumstance of a grand national convention may suggest to us. But, if you carry the distrust of the moment into futurity, have a care that, by dint of exaggerating our fears, we render not the preservatives worse than the very malady; and that, instead of uniting the citizens by the bond of freedom, we do not split them into two parties, ever ready to conspire one against the other. If, at every step we take, we be threatened with the resuscitation of departed despotism; if the dangers from a very minute part of the public force, be incessantly opposed as an objection, notwithstanding the millions of men who are in arms for the constitution, what other line of action then remains? Let us perish this very instant. Let us whelm the vaulted roofs of this temple

upon

upon our heads, and, to-day, expire freemen, if to-morrow we must be slaves *.

" We must, it is further said, restrain the use of the public force in the hands of the monarch; I think as you do, and we differ only as to the means. Beware, lest, in endeavouring to restrain his hands, you prevent them from acting altogether.

" But, according to the rigour of principles, can a state of war ever commence, without the nation's having determined upon the propriety of the measure?

" To this I answer: the interest of the nation is, that all hostility be repelled by him who hath the direction of the public force; this is what I understand by a state of war. The interest of a nation is, that the warlike preparations made by neighbouring powers, be ba-

---

* *Bravo!*—Might we not think that he here alluded to the death of Sampson? W.

lanced

lanced by preparations on our side; here again is the state of war, under another point of view. No deliberation can precede such events, such preparations. It is when hostility, or the necessity of defence by force of arms, which comprehends every case, shall be notified to the legislative body, that it will take the measures which I propose; it will approve or disapprove; it will request a negotiation of peace; it will grant or refuse the necessary supplies; it will impeach the ministers; it will arrange the internal force; it will confirm the treaty of peace, or will refuse to ratify it. I know but of this one mode, of allowing the legislative body a useful co-operation, in the exercise of the right of war and peace, that is, a mixt power, participating at once of action and of will.

" But will not the preparations also, which

which are to be left in the king's hands, become a dangerous inftrument? Undoubtedly they will; but it is a danger unavoidable in every fyftem. It is very evident, that, in order to concentrate, ufefully, in the legiflative body, the exclufive exercife of the right of war and peace, we muft leave it alfo the care of fuperintending the preparations. But can you do fo, without altering the form of government? And, if the king is to be charged with the preparations; if he is obliged, by the nature and extent of our poffeffions, to diftribute that warlike apparatus afar off, muft we not therefore allow him a great latitude in the means? Would not limiting the preparations be the fame thing as deftroying them? Now, I afk you, whether, when the preparations are in being, the commencement of the ftate of war depend on us, or upon

upon chance, or on the enemy? I afk you, whether, frequently, feveral battles fhall not have been fought, before the king can know a fyllable of the matter, before any fuch hoftile meafures can be notified to the nation?

" But, might not the legiflative body be allowed a concurrence in the preparations for a war, for the purpofe of diminifhing the danger of fuch preparations? Might not a committee of the National Affembly be appointed to keep an eye on them? Have a care, gentlemen; we fhould confound all the powers, by confounding action with will, direction with law; the executive power would ere long become only the agent of a committee; we fhould thus affume the function not only of legiflating, but likewife of governing; for what limits can you affign to this concurrence, to this fuperintendance?

ance? In vain would you affign any; in fpite of all your forecaft, they will every one be violated.

" Have a care too, with regard to another point. Are you not afraid of palfying the executive power, by this cooperation of means? In matters relative to execution, what is to be the work of many, is never well done by any. Befides, where, in fuch an order of things, are we to look for that refponfibility, which ought to be the ægis of our new conftitution?

" In fine, have we nothing to fear from a king, who, mafking his fchemes of defpotifm under the appearance of a neceffary war, fhould re-enter the kingdom at the head of a victorious army, not in order to refume his poft of king-citizen, but for the purpofe of re-poffeff-
ing

ing himself of the iron throne of tyranny *?

"Well then, what is likely to happen? I suppose, that a warrior-king and conqueror, uniting with military talents the vices which corrupt men, and the amiable qualities which captivate them, is not at all a prodigy, and that it behoves us, by sage laws, to provide against such prodigies.

"I go upon the supposition, that some corps of a national army, may not possess sufficient patriotism and virtue to resist a tyrant, and that such a king might find it as easy to lead the French against the French, as Cæsar did (and Cæsar was not born a king) to prevail upon a few Gauls to pass the Rubicon †.

* Mais pour reconquérir celui des tyrans.
† Aussi facilement que César, qui n'étoit pas né sur le trone, fît passer le Rubicon à des Gaulois.

"But

" But let me aſk you, whether this objection be not applicable to all the ſyſtems, and whether we ſhall never have need to arm a numerous public force, becauſe the excluſive exerciſe of the right of war and peace, ſhall be veſted in the legiſlative body?

" Let me aſk you, whether, by ſuch an objection, you are not preciſely introducing into monarchies, the inconveniences peculiar to republics? for, it is chiefly in popular governments that ſuch ſucceſſes are to be dreaded. It was amongſt nations which had no kings, that ſuch ſucceſſes paved the way to royalty. It was to Carthage, it was to Rome, that ſuch citizens as Hannibal and Cæſar, became dangerous. Wither the hopes of ambition, dry up her ſap, blaſt her*; let a monarch

---

* In two words, " Tariſſez l'ambition."—This is beating

monarch have nothing to figh for, but that in which the law can gratify him; make his magiftracy what it ought to be, and indulge no further fears, that a royal rebel, abdicating his crown, may run the rifk of hurrying from a victory to the fcaffold*.

beating a fmall bit of gold into leaf: it is unfurling a bright conception, and letting its ftrong colours be feen to beft advantage. Neverthelefs, the fublime delights in brevity. W.

* Here fome murmurs interrupted the orator. M. *Defprémenil* ftood up and faid: " I defire that M. Mirabeau be called to order; he is forgetting that the king's perfon hath been declared inviolable."

MIRABEAU.

" I fhall take care how I anfwer the charge of difloyalty preferred againft me: you have all heard the cafe that I was fuppofing, namely, that of a defpotic monarch who revolts againft his people, who comes home with an army of Frenchmen, to re-poffefs himfelf of the ftrong hold of tyranny: now, a king is, in fuch a cafe, a king no longer."—*The hall refounded with applaufe, and the orator proceeded*—

" It

" It were difficult, and even useless, to continue a debate, already but too long, amidst applause and disapprobation alike extravagant, alike unjust. I have spoken, because I deemed that it was not for me to dispense with speaking, upon an occasion of such importance. I have spoken according to my conscience and my opinion; I owe to this assembly only what I consider as truth, and I have uttered that truth. I have uttered it perhaps rather boldly, while wrestling with potent adversaries. I were unworthy of the office wherewith I am intrusted; I were unworthy of being numbered amongst the friends of liberty, should I dissemble my sentiments, while inclined to a middle party, between the opinion of those whom I love and hold in honour, and the counsels of men who have been most at variance with me, since the commencement of this assembly.

"You have grasped my system: it consists in assigning a concurrent exercise of the right of making war and peace, to the two powers which have been sanctioned by the constitution. I think I have combated, with advantage, the arguments likely to be adduced upon this question, in favour of the exclusive systems. There is but one unanswerable objection, which hath place in all their systems, and equally in mine, and which will ever embarrass the various questions, that shall touch upon the confusion of the powers; and that is, how to determine upon the means of obviating the last degree of the abuse. I know of but one: one, and but one, will be discovered, and I shall denote it by this trite, and perhaps

inelegant

inelegant allusion, which I have already allowed myself to make use of in this place, but which describes my idea exactly. It is *the alarm-bell of necessity*, which alone can give the signal, when the moment is arrived for fulfilling the imprescriptible duty of resistance; that duty ever imperious when the constitution hath been violated, ever triumphant when the resistance is just, and truly national*.

" I am now going to read to you my plan of the decree: it is not good, it is. incomplete. A decree upon the right of war and peace, will never truly become the moral code of the law of nations, until you shall have constitutionally organized the army, the fleet, the finances, your national guards, your colonies. It is my earnest desire, then, that gentlemen will

* *Bravo!*

perfect the scheme which I have drawn out, it is my desire that they will propose to us a better. I will not attempt to conceal the sentiments of diffidence, with which I present it to you; I will not conceal, too, my profound regret, that the man who hath laid the foundations of the constitution, and who hath contributed the most to your immortal work, that the man who hath revealed to the world the true principles of representative government, condemns himself to a silence which I deplore, which I esteem criminal, however ungratefully his immense services may have been repaid, that the Abbé Sieyes—I ask his pardon for naming him—does not himself advance to insert in the constitution, one of the greatest springs which actuate the state of civil polity. I am the more grieved at this dereliction,

liction, since, crushed under a weight far above my strength of intellect, incessantly called away by that recollection and meditation, which are the prime powers of man, I had not directed my attention to this question, accustomed as I was to rely upon that illustrious thinker*, for putting the last hand to his own admirable workmanship. I have pressed him, conjured him, entreated him as a suppliant, in the name of that friendship with which he honours me, in the name of patriotism, that sentiment otherwise so sacred and full of energy, to endow us† with his ideas, not to leave such a vast chasm in the constitution. He refused me; I tell it openly. I conjure you, however, to call

---

* Ce grand penseur.
† De nous doter de ses idées.

upon him for his opinion, which ought not to be kept secret; to tear, at length, from the arms of discouragement, a man whose silence and inaction I consider as a public calamity*.

"After this declaration, for the candour of which at least you will give me credit, if you will dispense with my reading my plan of the decree, I shall be grateful for the indulgence. [*Read, read.*] You are determined, then, that I shall read it: bear in mind that I do so in obedience to your command, and that I have had the courage to risk your displeasure, in my zeal to do you service.

"I move you to decree the following, as constitutional articles.

* I know of no passage in Cicero, of the complimentary kind, superior to this angry eulogium on the Abbé Sieyes. W.

Article I.

"The right of making war and peace belongs to the nation.

"The exercise of this right shall be delegated concurrently to the legislative body and the executive power, in the manner following:

"II. The care of watching over the external security of the empire, of maintaining its rights and its possessions, belongs to the king; accordingly, for him alone shall it be lawful to keep up political connections with foreign powers, conduct negotiations, make choice of the proper agents to be employed in such affairs, make warlike preparations proportioned to those made by the neighbouring states, distribute the forces by sea and land, in such manner as he shall deem expedient, and regulate the direction of them in case of war.

III. "In

"III. In the case of hostilities impending or commenced, of an ally to be supported, of a right to be asserted by force of arms, it shall be incumbent on the king to notify, without delay, such circumstance to the legislative body, to make known the causes and the motives, and to ask for the necessary supplies; and, should the necessity for such notification arise during the recess of the legislative body, that body shall be immediately re-assembled.

"IV. If, upon such notification, the legislative body deem, that the hostilities commenced are a criminal aggression on the part of ministry, or of some other agent of the executive power, the author of such aggression shall be impeached as guilty of treason against the nation; the National Assembly declaring, to that end,
that

that the French nation renounces conquest, of what kind soever it be, and that it will never employ its force against the liberty of any state.

" V. If, in case of the said notification, the legislative body refuse the necessary supplies, and manifest its disapprobation of the war, it shall be incumbent on the king to take such measures, immediately, as may prevent, or put a stop to all hostility, the ministers remaining responsible for delays.

" VI. The formulary of the declaration of war, and of the treaties of peace, shall be, ON THE PART OF THE KING OF THE FRENCH, AND IN THE NAME OF THE NATION.

" VII. In the case of an impending war, the legislative body shall extend its session into the customary intervals of recess, cefs, and may continue to fit, without any recefs, as long as the war shall endure.

"VIII. During the whole courfe of the war, it fhall be lawful for the legiflative body to requeft the executive power to negotiate a peace, and, in cafe the king fhall head the army in perfon, the legiflative body fhall have the right of affembling fuch a number of the national guards, and in fuch place, as it fhall deem expedient.

"IX. At the moment when the war fhall ceafe, the legiflative body fhall fix the fpace of time, within which the troops extraordinary fhall be difbanded, and the army reduced to the permanent eftablifhment; the pay of the faid troops fhall be continued no longer than to that fixed time, after which, fhould the troops extraordinary remain ftill embodied, the
minifter

minister shall be responsible, and be impeached as guilty of treason against the nation. To this end, it shall be incumbent on the committee of constitution, to consider forthwith of the mode of ministerial responsibility.

„ X. It belongs to the king to conclude and sign all treaties of peace, of alliance, and of commerce with foreign powers, and such other conventions as he shall deem consistent with the welfare of the state; but the said treaties and conventions shall become effective, only so far as they shall have been ratified by the legislative body*."

This speech obtained great applause. —It merited calumny.

JUNE

---

* In the course of this most able oration, the reader hath noticed what opinions were entertained

by

June 21, 1790.

M. *Barnave* at length made his appearance in the tribune, and, in a very well-made

by *Mirabeau*, with respect to certain parts of our unparalleled constitution. Those opinions are, doubtless, so many errors. It must, nevertheless, be owned, that *Mirabeau* hath handled in a very masterly manner, the grand question concerning the co-operation of the executive and legislative powers, which are the two main pillars of every constitution.

Let us hazard a concise assertion, and deliver it with philosophical solemnity. *The constitution of England will perish, when the legislative power shall have become more factious, than the executive is ambitious.* We know but too well, that it is not at all impossible, for a faction to possess itself of the seats in a legislative assembly, and, by some artful and audacious measure, arrayed in the garb of law, and by rendering the royal magistrate " a splendid cypher," to impose a new and unexpected domination upon the state.

made speech, appeared less to endeavour at offering a new opinion, than at combating

state. In Rome, the Agrarian law of the tribune *Rullus*, for vesting in ten persons, during the space of five years, an uncontrolled power of forming colonies of the poorer citizens, in such lands as belonged to the commonwealth by right of conquest, was one of the most insidious and, at the same time, daring *legal* projects, which had ever been attempted in favour of faction and ambition. Fortunately for Rome, it miscarried, by the eloquence and activity of *Cicero*.

A question might be started, whether, in the English Constitution, it were not better that there should exist an incessant opposition to ministry, even though that opposition be composed of a mere faction*, than that there should be no opposition

---

* Lord *Bolingbroke* hath well distinguished between *faction* and *party*. " Faction," says he, " depends upon the hopes of a few, Party upon the fears of the many "

whatever.

bating what had been advanced the day before by M. Mirabeau.—The reply of

whatever. I am inclined to the affirmative; but on this condition, that the people will be as watchful of the opposition as of the ministry. If it behoves us to be jealous of the executive power, it equally behoves us to be jealous of the legislative. Men are naturally induced to suspect the former; but they are also as naturally induced to pay a blind reverence to the latter, and to consider it as a friend incapable of wronging them.

With regard to the French affairs, one might venture to assert, that the final issue will depend on the respectability of the representative assembly; that is, upon vigilance co-operating with integrity. It was a fortunate circumstance for the exiled *Stuart* family, that the death of Charles I. was succeeded by an usurpation. For the people at length sickened, at the idea of having been betrayed from despotism to despotism. Had a regular, and legal republican form of government, taken place in England after the king's execution, it is highly probable that Monarchy would never again have shewn her face in this island. W.

the

the latter will shew, whether M. Barnave had been as just, as he had been seducing. He concluded with presenting the following dispositions:

"To the king, supreme depositary of the executive power, belongs the right of providing for the security of the frontiers, of protecting the national property, of making the necessary preparations, of directing the forces by sea and land, of commencing negotiations, of nominating embassadors, of signing treaties, of making to the legislative body, such propositions with respect to peace and war, as to him shall appear expedient; but the legislative body shall exclusively exercise the right of declaring war and peace, and of concluding treaties."

We think it useless to repeat, that, in

the course of giving his opinion, M. Barnave let fall several expressions offensive to Mirabeau; but what it becomes us to tell, is, that the discourse of M. Barnave produced a very great effect, and that part of the assembly called suddenly for the question, to be put upon the plan of decree which he had presented.

M. *Cazalés* desired that the debate should be adjourned to the morrow; but that, *on the morrow*, the discussion *should be closed.*

MIRABEAU.

" I ascend the tribune, in order to support the motion of the member who spoke last; but I call for an explanation of the words: *The discussion shall be closed.* The many, the great many members of this assembly,

assembly, who appear seduced, persuaded, or convinced, by the speech of M. Barnave, either believe that that speech will triumph over all reply, or they do not believe so. If they do believe so, I should imagine, that one may expect from the generosity of their admiration, that they will not dread a reply, and that they will leave us the liberty of answering objections; if they do not believe so, THEIR DUTY IS, TO LISTEN TO INSTRUCTION *.

" At the same time that I acknowledge a very considerable share of ability in the speech of M. Barnave, my opinion is, that his whole argumentation may be overturned, that he hath not stated the true points of difficulty, and that he hath

* Is not this paragraph much in the manner of the late Mr. *Flood?* W.

neglected either some of my arguments, or some of the points of view under which they were presented. I claim, at least, the right of replying in my turn.

"I demand, that the question be discussed again to-morrow, and that it be not determined until after, by a sentiment of confidence or distrust, the assembly shall have closed the discussion. [*Here some murmurs were heard.*] My principal argument at this moment, is, the very warmth displayed in opposition to my demand."

JUNE 22, 1790.

Before we come to analyse some opinions which precede the reply of Mirabeau to M. Barnave, it is a duty I owe to my readers, to relate certain facts of considerable importance.

The

The enemies of our orator went so far, as to misrepresent the system which he had supported in the foregoing debate. And the people, that is, some obscure men, who, according to a cruel custom among us, are called the people, had been wrought upon to such a degree, that even the life of Mirabeau was threatened*.

Already

---

* Mirabeau, upon this occasion, became the object of so many imputations and calumnies, that he thought it incumbent on him to submit both his Speech and his Reply, to the tribunal of all the departments. He accordingly ordered them to be printed, and the following was his epistle dedicatory:

To the Gentlemen Administrators of the Departments.

" Gentlemen,

" As long as they calumniated only my private life, I remained silent, either, because a rigid silence is a just expiation for faults purely personal, how-

Already an infamous libel was hawked through the streets of Paris, entitled: THE

ever excusable they might be, and I wished to be obliged to time alone, and to my services, for the esteem of those whose esteem is worth having*; or, still more, because I ever considered the rod of public censure as infinitely respectable, even when placed in the hands of my enemies; or, most of all, because I have been always of opinion, that it favours of narrow egotism and ridiculous inconsistency, to attempt to take up the time of one's fellow-citizens, with every thing but what concerns them.

"But, now that they attack me in my principles, as a public man, now that they menace the whole community in menacing my opinions, I could not stand aloof without deserting a post of honour, without violating, I may say, the precious deposit which hath been entrusted to me; and I think I owe a particular account of my belied opinion, to

* L'estime des gens de bien.

that

THE WHOLE DISCOVERY OF THE GRAND TREASON OF THE COUNT DE MIRABEAU. The authors, or the *pay-*

that very nation, whose interests I am accused of having betrayed. It is not enough for me, that the National Assembly hath washed away this odious imputation, by adopting my system almost with unanimity; I must also receive judgment from that tribunal, of which the legislator himself is only the servant and the organ. Such a judgment is the more important, since, placed hitherto amongst the useful tribunes of the people, I owe it a more strict account of my opinions. Such a judgment is the more necessary, since the question is, to pronounce on principles which distinguish the true theory of liberty from the false, her true apostles from false apostles, the friends of the people from its corruptors; for, in a free constitution, the people also hath its courtiers, its parasites, its flatterers, its slaves.

"During a solemn debate upon the exercise of the right of peace and war, while one part of the as-

pay-masters of this infernal production, had resolved to have it written for such as cannot

sembly was for preserving that right entire in the royalty, and another was for giving it exclusively to the legislative body, without the co-operation of the king; I proposed conferring that redoubted right, concurrently on the two parts, which compose the sovereign delegation of the nation.

" Examination soon re-united the members of the popular party, whose division upon that question arose merely from a mistake. But they who, desiring at any price to become heads of faction, rather than professors of opinion, had founded their hopes of success upon calumny and intrigue; they who, before they would even condescend to hear me, had rendered the very delivery of my speech a matter of peril; they who turned a principle of constitution into a question of self-interest, into an affair of party; those very persons, even after having been evidently vanquished upon the principles, thought proper to refuse their assent to them. They received, however, from the galleries, the applause which had been prepared for them; but their system, in appearance

cannot read; in fact, it was read by those who *cannot read*, and the danger of Mirabeau pearance more popular, and more adapted to affect the ignorant and unadvised multitude, could not obtain them fifty suffrages in the assembly below, which opposed its usual courage to menaces and seduction.

" It is to you, gentlemen, that I now submit my plan of decree and my two speeches; you will, doubtless, be afflicted to find, how far the spirit of party can alter the most important questions, and sow dissension amongst the most necessary auxiliaries of liberty. But did it become me, for the miserable triumph of a momentary success, to abandon the principle, which made the king's participation in the amount of the general will, one of the bases of our constitution? Did it become me to erect altars to popularity, as the ancients did to terrour, and, offering up to it my opinions and my duties, appease it by a criminal sacrifice?

" Those, gentlemen (already every enlightened citizen perceives it), those alone will be the true friends of the people, who will teach it, that the

emotions

rabeau augmented. The tree on which they had determined to sacrifice him was marked out.

The victim, on his arrival in the hall of the Assembly, was accosted by one of his colleagues in these words:—*Your opinion is*

emotions which have been necessary to upraise us from insignificance, should be succeeded by conceptions fit to organize us for the future; that, after having sufficiently sacrificed to jealousy, after having rid ourselves of the miserable rubbish, a universal concurrence of wills becomes requisite to rebuild; that, at length, it is time to pass from a state of lawful insurrection, to the durable tranquillity of true social order, and that the means which acquired liberty, are not those which must preserve it *.

I am with respect,
Gentlemen,
Your most humble
And most obedient Servant,
MIRABEAU the Elder.

Paris, July 1, 1790.

* Brave!

is just, it is favourable to the nation, and, nevertheless, you are accused, you are threatened. Here, read it; see what is now circulating about the streets of Paris; there is a conspiracy against your life. Be firm—

Mirabeau read the title of the accusation, which had been brought before the tribunal of the people. *I know it very well*, was the answer he made to his friend; *they shall carry me from the Assembly, triumphant or piece-meal.*

However, Messieurs d'Estourmel, Duquesnoi, Goupil, le Chapellier, and Duport, were heard successively. They all (M. Duport excepted) coincided pretty nearly in opinion with Mirabeau.

The man whom every eye was seeking, whom some hoped to find at fault, because he had had but a single night to prepare

for

for his reply; but whose success was wished for by the majority, because they knew his talents, and were satisfied of the justice of his cause; the man, who had come to the knowledge, but a few minutes before, of the plots laid against his reputation and his life, at length made his appearance in the tribune *.

* M. *Chapelier* had adopted the plan of decree presented by Mirabeau, and made thereto the following amendments. He drew up article V. in these terms: "*If, after the said notification, the legislative body decree that a war ought not to be entered into, it shall be incumbent on the executive power to take immediate measures for bringing about a cessation, or a prevention of hostilities; the ministry remaining responsible for delays.*"— He moved that article VII. should be referred to the Committee of Constitution.—He reduced article VIII. to these terms: "*During the whole course of the war, it shall be lawful for the legislative body to request the king to negotiate a peace.*" Mirabeau adopted all these amendments.

MIRABEAU.

"It is, doubtless, a point gained, towards reconciling opposite opinions, to make known clearly what it is that produces the coincidence, and what it is that constitutes the difference. Amicable discussions are more favourable to a right understanding of our respective sentiments, than defamatory insinuation, outrageous accusations, the animosities of rivalship, the machinations of cabal and malevolence. A report hath been spread abroad, for this week past, that that part of the National Assembly, which approves the concurrence of the royal will, in the exercise of the right of peace and war, hath incurred the guilt of parricide

parricide against public liberty. Rumours of perfidy, of corruption, are disseminated; popular vengeance is invoked to aid the tyranny of opinion. One might assert, that there cannot, without a crime, exist two opinions, upon one of the most delicate and most difficult questions of civil organization. What a strange madness this, what a deplorable blindness, which thus inflames us one against the other, men whom one and the same object, the same indestructible* sentiment, should, amidst the most fell debates, still reconcile, still re-unite; men, who substitute the irascibility of self-interest in place of patriotism, and deliver up one another to the rage of popular prejudice!

" As for me; but a few days past, it

* By good luck, and to my great astonishment, I found this word in Johnson's dictionary. W.

was proposed to carry me in triumph, and now, the cry is, through every street of Paris: THE GRAND TREASON OF THE COUNT DE MIRABEAU.—I did not want such a lesson, to inform me, that there is but a short distance from the Capitol to the Tarpeian rock. However, a man combating for reason, for his country, will not so readily acknowledge himself vanquished. He who feels within himself the conscioufness of having deserved well of his country, and, especially, of being still of use to it; he who does not feed upon a vain celebrity, and who contemns the success of a day, when looking forward to true glory; he who wishes to speak the truth, who hath at heart the public welfare, independently of the fickle movements of popular opinion; such a man bears along with him the recompense of

his

his services, the mitigation of his pains, and the price of all his perils; such a man must expect his harvest, his destiny, the only one which interests him, the destiny of his fame, from time alone, that judge incorruptible, who renders strict justice to every one. Let those, who, for this week past, have been prophesying my opinion, without knowing what it was, who, at this moment, are calumniating my speech without understanding it, let those accuse me of offering incense to idols without power, at the very moment when they lie prostrate, or of being the vile stipendiary, of men against whom I have indefatigably waged war; let them arraign as an enemy to the revolution, the man who, perhaps hath not been altogether useless to it, and who, were that revolution unconnected with his renown, might there alone expect

an

an afylum; let them deliver up to the fury of an infatuated people, the man who, for thefe twenty years, hath been the adverfary of oppreffion, who talked to the French of liberty, of conftitution, of refiftance, when his bafe calumniators were at nurfe in the court of defpotifm, and fuckled with the milk of overbearing prejudices*. What is all this to me? This treatment, thefe unworthy practices, fhall not arreft me in my career. I will fay to my antagonifts, anfwer, if you are able; then calumniate, as much as you pleafe †.

" I re-

---

* Suçoient le lait des cours, et vivoient de tous les préjugés dominans.

† Illuftrious paragraph!—What a torrent of fublime eloquence, what gallant indignation, what an animated difplay of glorious fervices, what a grand and courageous confcioufnefs of patriotifm!—Affuredly, the noble orator had amply imbibed the fpirit

"I re-enter the lifts, then, with no armour but my principles, and the fortitude of confcience. I am going to ftate, in my turn, the real point of difficulty, with all the accuracy in my power; and I befeech fuch of my adverfaries as fhall not underftand me, to call on me to ftop, that I may exprefs myfelf more clearly; for, as to the reiterated reproaches of evafion, of fubtilty, of doubling and winding, I have refolved to fhake them off, " like dew-drops from the lion's mane*." As

of antiquity, " while his adverfaries were fucking the milk of defpotifm." He who feeks for any thing equal to this paragraph, muft look for it in the famed oration of Demofthenes *on the crown*, where that ftatefman defends his whole political life and character. Well may the friend and editor of *Mirabeau* exclaim; that thefe fpeeches " will inftruct orators yet unborn." W.

* I afk pardon for intruding this; there is nothing in the original to warrant it. W.

far

far as on me depends, this day shall unveil the secret of our respective loyalties. M. Barnave hath done me the honour to answer me alone; I mean to pay the same compliment to his talents; I am going to endeavour, in my turn, to refute him.

"You have said: we have instituted two distinct powers, the legislative and the executive; the one is commissioned to express the national will, the other to execute it. These two powers ought never to be confounded.

"You have applied these principles to the question of debate, that is, to the exercise of the right of war and peace.

"You have said: we must distinguish between action and will; action shall be the king's, will the property of the legislative body. Therefore, when the question shall be to declare war, such declaration being an act of will, it shall be the province

province of the legiflative body to make it.

"After having laid down this principle, you applied it to each article of my decree. I fhall follow the fame route; I fhall firft difcufs the general principle: I fhall then examine the application which you have made of it to the exercife of the right of war and peace: laftly, I mean to follow you ftep by ftep, in your criticifm on my decree.

"You affert, that we have two diftinct delegates, the one for action, the other for will: I deny it.

"The executive power, in whatever relates to action, is certainly very diftinct from the legiflative: but it is not true, that the legiflative body is entirely independant of the executive power, even when it is expreffing the general will.

"In fact, what is the organ of that general

neral will, according to the conſtitution? It is, at once, the aſſembly of the national repreſentatives, or the legiſlative body, and the repreſentative of the executive power; and it takes place in the manner following: the legiſlative body deliberates, and declares the general will; the repreſentative of the executive power hath the twofold right, either of ſanctioning the reſolution of the legiſlative body, and ſuch ſanction conſummates the law; or of exerciſing the *veto* which is granted to it for a certain time; and the conſtitution hath determined, that, during this period, the reſolution of the legiſlative body ſhould not be law. It is, therefore, inaccurate to ſay, that our conſtitution hath eſtabliſhed two delegates entirely diſtinct, even when the queſtion relates to the expreſſion of the general will. On the contrary, we have

have two reprefentatives, who co-operate in the formation of law, one of whom introduces a kind of fecondary will, exercifes over the other a fpecies of controul, and beftows on the law his fhare of influence and authority. Therefore, the general will does not refult, from the uncompounded will * of the legiflative body.

" Let us now purfue the application of your principle, to the exercife of the right of war and peace.

" You have faid: whatever, in this, is nothing more than will, as in all the reft, returns to its natural principle, and can be declared by the legiflative power alone. Here I ftop you; and I difcover your fophifm in a fingle word, which you yourfelf have brought forward: you fhall not, then, efcape from me.

* La fimple volonté.

" In

"In your speech, you confer exclusively the enunciation of the general will—upon whom? *Upon the legiſlative power;* upon whom do you confer it in your decree? *Upon the legiſlative body.* And for this, I call you to order. You have *forfeited* the conſtitution. If you mean, that the legiſlative body is the legiſlative power, you thereby overturn every law that we have made; if, whenever the queſtion turns upon expreſſing the general will, with reſpect to war, the legiſlative body ſuffices—According to that alone, the king having neither participation, nor influence, nor controul, nor any thing of all that we have granted to the executive power, by our ſocial ſyſtem, you would have, in legiſlation, two different principles; the one for ordinary legiſlation, the other for legiſlation with reſpect to war, that is, for the most terrible crisis which can agitate the body politic; one while you would have need, and another while you would have no need, of the assistance of the monarch, in order to express the general will—and you it is, who talk of homogeneousness, of unity, of compactness* in the constitution! Attempt not to say, that this distinction is idle; it is so little entitled to that epithet, it is so important in my eyes, and in the eyes of every good citizen who countenances my doctrine, that, if you will substitute, in your decree, in place of the words, *the legislative body*, these words, *the legislative power*, and define that power thus: An act of the National Assembly, sanctioned by the king, we shall, by that alone, come to an agreement upon the principles; but you will then return

* D'ensemble.

to my decree, becaufe it grants lefs to the king—You make no anfwer—I proceed.

" This contradiction becomes ftill more ftriking, in the application which you yourfelf have made of your principle, to the cafe of a declaration of war.

" You have faid: a declaration of war is no more than an act of will; therefore, it is the province of the legiflative body to exprefs it.

" I have here two queftions to put to you, each of which involves two different cafes.

" The firft queftion is; do you mean that the declaration of war is fo far the property of the legiflative body, that the king hath not the initiative, or do you mean that he hath the initiative?

" In the former cafe, if he hath not the initiative, do you mean likewife that
he

he hath not the *veto?* From that moment the king is without co-operation, in the moſt important act of the national will. How do you reconcile this with the rights which the conſtitution hath conferred upon the monarch? How do you reconcile it with the public intereſt? You will have as many encouragers of war, as there ſhall be men of fiery temper.

" Are there, or not, great inconveniencies in ſuch an order of things? You do not deny that there are.

" Are there any, on the contrary, in allowing the king the initiative? By the initiative, I mean a notification, any meſſage whatſoever? You cannot diſcover any inconvenience there.

" Obſerve, moreover, the natural courſe of things. In order to deliberate, it is neceſſary to be informed; by whom are you to be informed, if not by him who

who hath the superintendance of your foreign connections?

" That were, indeed, a strange constitution, which, having conferred upon the king the supreme executive power, should provide a mean of declaring war, without the king's having originated the debate upon that subject, in consequence of those connections which it is his duty to maintain; your assembly were no longer a deliberating, but an acting body; it were, in fact, the governing power.

" You will, therefore, allow the initiative to the king.

" Let us now proceed to the second case.

" If you allow the king the initiative, either, you suppose that it is to consist in a mere notification, or you suppose, that the king will declare which side it is his inclination to take.

" If

"If the king's initiative muft be confined to a fimple notification, the king, in fact, will have no concurrence in the declaration of war.

" If, on the contrary, the king's initiative confift, in a declaration of the courfe which he thinks ought to be taken, you have here a double hypothefis, upon which I requeft that we may argue.

" Do you mean that, when the king fhall have given his vote for war, the legiflative body may deliberate upon peace? I find no inconvenience here. Do you mean, on the contrary, that, when the king is inclined to peace, it fhall be lawful for the legiflative body to order war, and to caufe it to be carried on in fpite of him? I cannot adopt your fyftem, because here arife inconveniencies which it is not poffible to remedy.

" From this war determined on in fpite

of the king, would ere long refult a war of opinion, againft the king, againft all his agents. The moft turbulent fuperintendancy would prefide over all the operations; the defire of feconding thofe operations, diftruft of the miniftry, would betray the legiflative body to tranfgrefs its proper limits. Committees of military execution would be propofed, as fome have lately propofed committees of political execution; the king would be then no more than the agent of thefe committees; we fhould have two executive powers, or rather the legiflative body would exercife the royalty.

" Therefore, by this encroachment of one power upon the other, our conftitution would utterly depart from its own nature; from being monarchical, as it ought to be, it would become a downright ariftocracy. You have not anfwered

swered this objection, and I think that you never can answer it. You talk of restraining nothing but ministerial abuses, and I am talking of the means of restraining the abuses of a representative assembly; I am telling you, that it is our duty to controul that bias, which all government takes insensibly towards the predominating form, wherewith it is impressed.

"If, on the contrary, when the king is inclined to war, you confine the deliberations of the legislative body, to a consent that such war shall be undertaken, or to a resolution that it ought not to be undertaken, and to compelling the executive power to negotiate a peace, you avoid all those inconveniencies: and take especial notice (for here it is that my system is so eminently distinguished), that you are perfectly consistent with the principles of the constitution.

"The

"The king's *veto* finds itself, from the very nature of things, almoft entirely blunted in affairs of execution; rarely can it take place in matters relative to war. You parry this inconvenience; you re-eftablifh the fuperintendancy, the reciprocal controul, which the conftitution hath provided, in impofing upon the two delegates of the nation, her removable reprefentatives, and her unremovable reprefentative, the mutual duty of coinciding, when the queftion is upon war. You attribute likewife to the legiflative body, the fole faculty which can enable it to concur, without inconvenience, in the exercife of this terrible privilege. You at the fame time fecure the national intereft, as far as in you lies; fince all that you will have to do, in order to arreft the progrefs of the executive power, will be, to require it to place

place continually within the reach of the legiſlative body, the means of deliberating on every caſe which can preſent itſelf.

"It appears to me, gentlemen, that the point of difficulty is at length completely known; and, for a man for whom ſuch applauſe was prepared within and without doors, M. Barnave hath not at all approached the true ſtate of the queſtion. It were now but too eaſy a triumph, to purſue him through all the particulars, where, if he hath exhibited the talents of a ſpeaker, he hath not betrayed the ſlighteſt ſymptoms of a ſtateſman, nor any knowledge of human affairs*. He hath declaimed againſt the mischiefs

---

* Wonderful man yourſelf!—after having ſeen you diſplay ſuch high powers of declamation, we now find you reaſoning with the cloſeneſs of an
Ariſtotle,

mischiefs which kings can do, and which they have done; and he hath taken special care not to remark, that, in our constitution, the monarch can never hereafter assume the character of a despot, nor do any thing that can be interpreted as arbitrary. And above all, he hath taken good care not to speak of popular emotions, although he himself could have given an example, of the facility with which the friends of a foreign power, can influence the opinion of a national assembly, by collecting the people around it, and by procuring for their agents, in the public walks, a clapping of hands, as a testimony of general favour. He hath quoted

Aristotle, with the candour of a *Fenelon*. Yet (and here you rise above the generality of men of argument), the dignity of the orator pursues you even in your logic; you syllogize with an air of majesty. W.

Pericles

Pericles involving his country in a war, in order to avoid paffing his accounts; fhould not one be led to imagine, on hearing M. Barnave, that Pericles was a king, or a defpotic minifter? Pericles was a man, who, well knowing how to flatter the paffions of the people, and to procure feafonable applaufe when defcending from the tribune, by his largeffes, or by thofe of his friends, plunged into the Peloponnefian war—whom? The national affembly of Athens.

" I come now to the critique upon the plan of my decree, and fhall take a rapid review of the different objections.

" Article the firft. *That the right of making war and peace belongs to the nation.*

" M. Barnave maintains that this article is ufelefs; why ufelefs? We have not delegated

delegated the royalty, we have recognized it, as exifting anterior to the conftitution. Now, fince it hath been maintained in this affembly, that the right of making war and peace is inherent in the kingly office, fince it hath been afferted, that we have not even the power of delegating that right, I was therefore warranted, it was my duty to declare in my decree, that the right of war and peace was the property of the nation. Where, then, is the fnare?

"Article the fecond. '*That the exercife of the right of war and peace, ought to be delegated concurrently to the legiflative body, and the executive power, in the manner following.*' According to M. Barnave, this article is contrary to the principles, and difcovers the fallacy in my decree. Such is, in fact, the queftion, the true question which agitates us. Speak accurately; ought the two delegates of the nation co-operate, or not, in expressing the general will? If they ought, can we assign to one of them an exclusive delegation in the exercise of the right of war and peace? Compare my article with yours; you mention neither the initiative properly so called, nor proposition, nor sanction on the part of the king. If no more do I speak, either of proposition or of sanction, I compensate for this concurrence by another. The line which separates us is, therefore, well known: it is I who am in the constitution, it is you who are departing from it. It is very necessary that you should return to it. Whereabouts is the snare?

" It consists, you say, in my not expressing in what manner the concurrence
of

of those two delegates should be exercised. What? not express it! Then, what do these words signify: *in the manner following*; and what is the object of the articles which follow? Have I not said precisely, in several of the articles, that the notification is in the king, and the resolution, the approbation, the disapprobation, in the National Assembly? Does it not evidently result from each of my articles, that it never shall be lawful for the king to commence a war, nor even to continue it, without the determination of the legislative body? Where is the snare? I know of but one snare in this discussion; that of having affected to give the legislative body no more than the decision upon war and peace, and of having, nevertheless, in fact, by means of a mental reservation *,

* Une réticence.

a deception of words, entirely excluded the king from all participation, from all influence, in the exercife of the right of peace and war.

"I know of but one fnare in this bufinefs; but here a little aukwardnefs hath revealed your fecret: it is this; in diftinguifhing the declaration of war in the exercife of the right, as an act of mere will, you have confequently appropriated it to the legiflative body only; as if the legiflative body, which is not the legiflative power, had, without the king's concurrence, the exclufive property of the will!

"Article the third. Here we perfectly agree.

"Article the fourth. You have afferted, that I had required the notification, only in cafe of fome hoftility; that I had taken for granted that every act of hoftility
was

was a war; and that, accordingly, I permitted the executive power to make war, without the co-operation of the legiflative body. How unfair! I have required the notification to be made, in the cafe of *hoftilities impending or commenced, of an ally to be fupported, of a right to be preferved by force of arms:* have I, or not, comprehended all the cafes? Where is the fnare?

" I have faid in my fpeech, that hoftilities often preceded deliberation; I have faid, that thofe hoftilities might be of fuch a nature, as to amount to a commencement of the ftate of war. What anfwer have you made me? That war could exift no otherwife than by a declaration of war. But, are we difputing about things, or about words? You have faid with ferioufnefs, what M. de Bougainville faid at the feafight of the Grenades, in a moment of heroic gaiety; the bullets were flying about his ship; he cried out to his officers: *The pleasant thing is, gentlemen, that all this while we are not at war*; and, in fact, war had not been declared.

"You have gone largely into the present case of Spain. An act of hostility hath been committed: would the National Assembly of Spain have no occasion for deliberation? Doubtless it would, and I have said so, and my decree hath formally provided for the case; here are hostilities commenced, a right to be maintained, a war impending. You have concluded, then, that an act of hostility does not constitute a state of war. But if, instead of two vessels taken and released in Nootka Sound, there had been an engagement between two ships of war; if, in order to support them, two squadrons had intermeddled

meddled in the quarrel; if an enterprifing admiral had purfued the vanquifhed into port; if an ifland of fome importance had been taken, would there not then have exifted a ftate of war? This will be all that you defire; but fince neither your decree, nor mine, prefents means of making the deliberations of the legiflative body take the lead of fuch hoftilities, you will admit that it is not there the queftion lies. But where is the fnare?

" Article the fifth. It hath been my wifh to make mention of a poffible fact, a fact, of which you, in your decree, do not feem to be in the leaft aware. In the cafe of hoftilities received and repulfed, there may exift a blameable aggreffion; the nation ought to have the right of impeaching and punifhing the author of it. It is not fufficient not to be engaged then

in

in war; we must restrain the person, who, by an imprudent or a perfidious step, would have risked or attempted engaging us in a war. I point out the means of doing it: do you call that a snare? But, according to you, I suppose that the executive power hath the right of commencing hostilities, of becoming an aggressor. No, I do not give it such a right, since I formally take away the right from it; I am not permitting aggression, for I am proposing to punish it. What, then, am I doing? I am reasoning upon a possible fact, one which neither you nor I can prevent. I cannot hinder the supreme depositary of the whole national force, from possessing mighty means and opportunities of abusing it; but is not this inconvenience to be found in every system? It shall be, if you like, the royal

distem-

distemper*: but do you pretend to assert, that a mere human institution, a government made by men, made for men, should be exempt from inconveniences? Do you pretend to maintain, that, because royalty hath its dangers, we must renounce its advantages? Out with it at once†; for then we shall have to determine, whether, because the fire burns, we should deprive ourselves of the warmth, and of the light which we obtain from it. All can hold good, excepting inconclusiveness; tell us, that we ought not to have any king; do not tell us that we ought to have only a powerless, a useless one.

"The sixth, seventh, and eighth arti-

---

* Le mal de la royauté.—I might have called it *The King's Evil*, but that would have appeared a pun. W.

† Dites-le nettement.

eles, I think you have not attacked; we are agreed, therefore, as to them. But allow, that he who imposes on the executive power, limitations which no other decree hath suggested, hath not complimented* the royal power with usurpation, as some have not scrupled to infist. Admit that he, as well as another, knows how to fortify the people's rights with constitutional precautions: admit that, at the very moment when that misled people is threatening him, he is combating for that people far better even than you†.

"Article the ninth. That in case the king shall head the army in person, the legislative body shall have the right of assembling such a number of the national guards, and in such place, as it shall deem

* Doté. † *Bravo!*

expedient.

expedient.—This measure hath drawn upon me your bitterest reproaches. It hath its inconveniences, undoubtedly; is there any institution which hath not? Had you thoroughly comprehended it, you would have perceived, that, had this measure been, as you have asserted, a needful accessory to my system, I should not have confined myself to applying it to the case, doubtless a very rare one, where the king headed the army in person*, but should have pointed it out as a remedy, for every case of war indefinitely. If, in all this, there be any snare, the snare lies entirely in your own mode of reasoning, and not in the system of one whose intention surely is, to keep the king aloof † from the command of armies beyond the

---

* Feroit la guerre en personne.
† Ecarter le roi.

frontiers,

frontiers, becauſe he does not think it meet, that the grand overſeer of the community ſhould be made the common centre of ſo many dangerous functions; the ſnare is not to be found in the ſyſtem of one, who provides your civil organization with the only mean of regular inſurrection, which decides the principles of your conſtitution. There is a manifeſt unfairneſs, in ranſacking my ſyſtem for weak points*, or for artful views in providing againſt an inconvenience, ſuggeſted by every member who hath ſpoken before me, and which exiſts alike in all the theories: for it is evident, that a martial monarch may be led aſtray by his paſſions, and ſeconded by legions educated in the ſchool of victory, whether the legiſlative, or the executive power have originated the

---

* A chercher la foibleſſe de mon ſyſtême.

war.

war: If, in every conftitutional hypothefis, this terrible mifchief can be equally forefeen, there is one remedy, and but one, to oppofe to it; you and I equally acknowledge the duty of infurrection, in certain extreme cafes infinitely rare. Is it fo culpable a provifion, to render infurrection more methodical and more formidable? Is it a fnare, to have affigned to the national guards their true deftination? And what are thefe troops, if they are not the troops of liberty? Wherefore have we inftituted them, if they be not deftined to the perpetual confervation of their conqueft?—But further; you were the firft among us who exaggerated this danger; either it exifts, or it does not exift; if it does not exift, why have you treated it as a thing of confequence? if it does exift, both my fyftem and yours are equally

equally threatened by it*. The cafe, then, being fo, either accept the mean I offer, or give me one inftead of it, or confent to go without any; it is all equal to me, to me who view this danger in the light only of a prodigy. I give my vote, therefore, for the amendments made by M. Chapelier, who is for leaving out this article.

"It is full time to terminate this long debate. I am in hope that, henceforward, none will think of fhutting their eyes againft the true point of difficulty. I am for the co-operation of the executive power, in the expreffing the general will with refpect to war and peace, in like manner as the conftitution hath conferred on it that co-operation, in every part already eftablifhed of our new focial fyf-tem.

---

* How like *Flood!*

tem.—My adversaries are not for it. I am contending, that the superintendance of one of the people's delegates, should never desert it* in the most important political operations; and my antagonists contend, that one of the delegates should exclusively possess the right of making war; as if, even were the executive power a stranger to the composition of the general will, our deliberations turned only on the declaration of war, and the exercise of the right involved not a series of mixt operations, in which action and will justle each other, and are confounded.

" Such, then, is the line which separates us. If I am mistaken, once again, let my adversary arrest me in my career, or rather let him substitute, in his decree, in

---

* See the grammatical note at the end of this debate. W.

place of these words, *the legislative body,* the words, *legislative power*, that is, an act issuing from the representatives of the nation, and sanctioned by the king, and we are perfectly agreed, if not in practice, at least in theory; and we shall then be able to judge, whether this theory be not better realized, in my decree than in any other.

"It hath been proposed to you, to decide the question, by a parallel between those who support the affirmative and the negative. You have been told, that you would see, on the one side, men who hope either for advancement in the army, or to be employed in transacting foreign affairs; men connected with the ministers and their agents; on the other, *the peaceful citizen, virtuous, unknown, unambitious, who finds his own happiness and existence,*

existence, in the happiness and existence of the community.

" I mean not to follow this example. I think, that it is no more conformable to the expediencies of politics, than it is to the principles of morality, to sharpen the poniard with which one cannot wound one's rival, without soon feeling the weapon returned upon one's own heart. I do not think that men, who ought to serve the public cause, as true brother soldiers, find any pleasure in fighting one another like vile gladiators; in striving for the mastery in defamation and intrigue, and not in information and talents; in seeking guilty triumphs in mutual ruin and depression, the trophies of a day, injurious to all, and even to the cause of glory. But I will tell you: amongst those who maintain my doctrine, you may reckon upon all men of moderation, who do not think that wifdom is to be found in extremes, not that the fpirit of pulling down fhould never make room for that of building up; you may reckon upon the greateft part of thofe energetic citizens, who, at the commencement of the States-General (fuch at that time was the appellation of this national convention, which is yet but in the cradle of liberty), trampled on fo many prejudices, braved fo many dangers, beat down fo many impediments, in order to make their way into the midft of the Commons, in whom that devotednefs infpired the courage and the force, which have really effectuated your glorious revolution; you will there behold thofe tribunes of the people, whom the nation will long rank amongft the number of her deliverers, notwithftanding the

inceffant

incessant barking of envious mediocrity; you will there see persons, whose very name disarms calumny, and whose reputation, both as public and private men, the most headstrong libellers have never essayed to tarnish; men, in fine, who without blemish, without views of interest, and without fear, will be honoured even to the grave, both by their friends and by their enemies*.

" I conclude with moving you, that my plan of decree be debated, as amended by M. Chapellier."

Mirabeau is not to depart *piece-meal* from the Assembly; he hath just now obtained the most complete *triumph:* applause almost unanimous hath informed him, that he had convinced even the greater part of those who decried his sys-

---

* *Bravo!*

tem.—The cry of *question* is heard from every side of the hall.—A decree proclaims that the discussion is at an end—Neverthelefs, Mirabeau is for hearing M. Barnave. Leave is obtained for that gentleman to speak—But M. Barnave is far from displaying, in his reply, the same ability for which his former speech had been distinguished—The preference is demanded for the plan of Mirabeau, who is powerfully supported by M. de la Fayette.—And the plan of Mirabeau does obtain the preference.

M. *Freteau* desires the following amendment in the first article.—*The right of peace and war belongs to the nation: it shall not be lawful to determine upon war, otherwise than by a decree of the National Assembly, which decree it shall not be lawful to to resolve, unless in consequence of a formal proposition from the king.*

MIRABEAU.

"M. Freteau hath drawn a false conclusion from my article, if he hath inferred from it, that it left the ministers the right of commencing war. That article foresees the case, where a minister might order a culpable aggression, or act of hostility. It is absolutely impossible to prevent such cases. It is extremely possible, that there should exist a minister, perverse enough to commence an underhand war. I ask, is there any system wholly free from this inconvenience? I can take no other precautions, than those which I point out, in enabling you to decide whether the aggression be a guilty one.

Does not the article clearly say so?—But why is there no answer given to the question which I have propounded? Is the legislative power the legislative body? Is it not, on the contrary, composed of the legislative body deliberating, and of the king consenting and sanctioning? The answer ought to be: *that, that* is the principle* of the system to which you have just given the preference."

The previous question is called for, upon the amendment of M. Freteau.

MIRABEAU.

" I declare that I am not one of those who call for the previous question; but I must observe, that the sense of M. Freteau's amendment is clearly expressed in my article."

---

* C'est là le principe, &c.

M. *de*

M. de Menou.—" M. Mirabeau says, that the amendment proposed by M. Freteau, is comprehended in his decree. If it be not comprehended in it, as I am tempted to believe, it should be made a separate article. I wish to divide the Assembly upon this amendment, which ought to have been formed into an article."

MIRABEAU.

" It is necessary to examine into the motive of this long-continued obstinacy, against seeing in my decree what is in it, and in pretending that I have said what I have not said. If the numerical order of my articles is to be changed, I leave the honour and glory of a discovery so sublime, to any who may have a mind to take possession of it. As the fifth article contains precisely the principle; as there is not a single article which does not suppose the principle; as there is not one of them which does not say, that the king is to pay obedience to the legislative body; as not one of my arrangements, none of my articles is equivocal, you will allow me to persist in not changing my opinion, in compliment to those worthy persons, who, for these two hours, have been endeavouring to make the public believe, that my opinion is not my opinion." [*Loud applause.*]

M. *Freteau* presents the first article, as thus drawn up by himself:—" The right of peace and war belongs to the nation: it shall not be lawful to determine upon war, otherwise than by a decree of the National Assembly, which shall be resolved upon, in consequence of the formal and
necessary

necessary proposition of the king, and which shall be consented to by him."

MIRABEAU.

"It will readily be believed, that I assent with all my heart to this amendment, for which I have been combating these five days. Had I known sooner, that this was only a contest of self-love, the discussion should have been much shorter than it hath been. I move you, that the word *sanctioned*, a constitutional word, be inserted instead of the word *consented*."

The articles were put successively to the vote, and the decree drawn up accordingly*.

* After this, in the original, follows a copy of the decree, containing the amendments agreed to. I omit translating it, as the reader, probably, begins to be weary of this debate. I shall therefore conclude with the additional article, proposed by M. Mirabeau. W.

May

May 24, 1790.

The journal of the proceedings of the 22d was read.

MIRABEAU.

" I propose an additional article to the decree which you have passed, upon the right of war and peace: it establishes a wish that hath been several times declared, by such of my colleagues as are sincerely attached to the cause of the people:—The article is, as follows:

" All treaties and conventions hitherto made with foreign powers or states, in the name of the king, shall be examined by a special committee of persons chosen by scrutiny, in this assembly, which committee shall, before the end of the present session, make its report upon each, to the end that the assembly may determine upon those, which it shall deem worthy of being ratified; and until then, the said treaties, acts, or conventions, are to remain in full force."

M. *Freteau* considers this plan of decree as a downright declaration of war; he moves the question of adjournment.

M. *Roberspierre*, on the contrary, looks upon this new article as a necessary consequence, of the decree resolved upon two days before; nevertheless, he consents to the adjournment.

MIRABEAU.

" An adjournment is, incontestably, at all times, a sage motion, especially when the question relates to some article of importance, and which, for that very reason, requires to be drawn up with much accuracy.

curacy. I muſt, however, remark, that the article bears altogether upon this principle, that henceforward it ſhall not be lawful to execute any thing, which hath not been firſt ratified by the legiſlative body. The events which happen every day, preſent us with opportunities of examining the conventions, which occaſion or call forth the diſplay of the national force. For example; although we are perſuaded, that the war between Spain and England is neither menacing nor dangerous; there is no doubt that it behoves us to look behind, and examine whether the conventions be national or not. I have therefore propoſed what I think uſeful to be done, antecedently to the cloſe of the ſeſſion; I agree to the adjournment; but my opinion is, that it ſhould be a ſhort one."

It

It was obferved by fome members, that the adjournment, like the decree, would amount to a declaration of war, fince it would create in foreign powers an apprehenfion of a revifion, of which it was impoffible for them not to entertain a jealoufy.

The affembly came to the refolution of paffing to the order of the day.

It had been, however, the intention of Mirabeau, in fuggefting the article already noticed, to introduce the following one:

"The affembly excepts from the claufe above-mentioned, every treaty, act, or convention, by which there may have been ftipulated, in behalf of any foreign power, a right of interfering in the internal affairs of the French nation, or in behalf of this nation, a like right of interfering in the internal affairs of any other power or state whatsoever: which said treaties, acts, or conventions, are here declared to be null and incapable of taking effect, as being contrary to the rights of nations, and to the principles of justice which should form the basis of their policy; the assembly declaring, that the nation will consider as inimical, every power which, in contempt of this declaration, shall interfere, in any shape whatsoever, in any matter appertaining to the legislation, or to the constitution of the French empire, such as it hath been, or shall be established, by the National Assembly, and accepted by the king."

Assuredly, this new article, had it been adopted, as it ought to have been, would have saved us the shame and trouble of making many bravadoes, and throwing out many threats, which, without
inti-

intimidating any one, ferved to caft a damp upon the activity of our commerce and our induſtry*.

FUNE-

* In one of the foregoing pages, I referred the reader to a note at the end of this debate; the note is relative to a point of Engliſh grammar, the mention of which I deemed it better to defer till now, in order to avoid diſturbing the attention of the reader from the ſubject then before him. The point alluded to is the uſing the word *it*, as a pronoun relative to the ſubſtantive *people*. This ſtartles many; becauſe we have indulged ourſelves in the cuſtom of confidering the word *people* as of the plural number, and, confequently, of connecting it with plural verbs and pronouns. I have heard it well obſerved, that nouns of multitude are the reproach of Engliſh grammar. The applying a plural verb to them, is a barbariſm that was unknown to the Greek and Roman languages, and is ſtill baniſhed from thoſe modern tongues, which are evidently a corruption of that of ancient Rome. Still leſs did thoſe elegant and well-organized languages, admit of a plural pronoun be-

FUNERAL EULOGIUM ON FRANKLIN.

June 11, 1790.

For several days, Mirabeau, tormented by a cruel disorder in his eyes, had not made his appearance in the assembly; and the

ing connected with the term, by which they denominated what we now call *the people*. The rule is uniformly the same, not only as to the number, but also as to the *gender* of that important appellation, in every one of the languages just mentioned. I appeal to the learned reader, with regard to the two first, and to the fashionable reader, with regard to all the rest. As to the gender, it was universally masculine. The λαος of the Greeks, the *populus* of the Latins, the *le peuple* of the French, the *il popolo* of the Italians, and the *lo peublo* of the Spaniards, form a respectable confederacy in behalf of my assertion. It is stated by those who are learned in our language, that all our words, which are not positively distinguished

the absence of Mirabeau was a public misfortune.

The guished as belonging to some sex, are necessarily degraded into the rabble of the neuter gender. Of which sex is the word *people*? Is it masculine? *he*, the people. Is it feminine? *she*, the people. Neither. Therefore, according to the rule laid down above, the word *people* must be a noun belonging to the neuter gender. Some of our most correct writers, aware of the impropriety of considering the word people as entitled to a plural verb, have imitated the purity of classical antiquity; but, with respect to the pronoun relating to the word people, they still adhere to the irregularity observed in common speech. For instance:—" The people *was* satisfied with the concessions made in *their* favour, and considered *themselves* secured from future encroachment."—The ancients spoke of *the people*, as of one great mass, that is, the nation, or, as one great portion of the general mass, in contradistinction to the aristocracy. With respect to the pronoun *it*, the universal objection is, that the ear is hurt, when that neuter pronoun re-

The father of the American revolution is no more. The Congress commissions M. de Rochefoucault to acquaint Mirabeau of this event.—Mirabeau is all affliction; his heart mourns, but he resolves not to be the only mourner; he thinks that all mankind should weep along with him.—He hath appeared in the assembly, asked leave to speak, interrupted the order of the day, and already obtained

presents the word *people:* very likely; so was my ear hurt, at first; but I disdained to compliment my ear by affronting my understanding. I recollect a dialogue in *Lucian*, called *the Judgment of the Vowels.* I wish some able grammarians would go the circuit of our language, and oblige those outlaws, those wandering banditti of pronouns and nouns of multitude, to forsake their irregular courses, and submit to the same government, under which all the other parts of speech are so happy. W.

the most delightful of all triumphs, A PRO-
FOUND AND PERFECT SILENCE.

MIRABEAU.

" Franklin is dead*.—The genius who freed America, and poured a copious stream of knowledge † throughout Europe, is returned into the bosom of the Divinity.

" The sage to whom two worlds lay claim, the man for whom science and politics are disputing, indubitably enjoyed an elevated rank in human nature.

" The cabinets of princes have been long in the habit of notifying, the death of those who were great only in their fu-

---

*"An instance of the sublime.—" Portia's dead."
—See *Smith*'s notes upon *Longinus*. W.

† Des torrens de lumière.—This is bad.

neral orations. Long hath the etiquette of courts proclaimed the mourning of hypocrify. Nations fhould wear mourning for none but their benefactors. The reprefentatives of nations fhould recommend to public homage, only thofe who have been the heroes of humanity.

" The Congrefs hath ordered, in the fourteen confederate ftates, a mourning of two months for the death of Benjamin Franklin; and America is, at this moment, paying that tribute of veneration, to one of the fathers of her conftitution.

" Were it not worthy of us, gentlemen, to join in this religious act, to pay our fhare of that homage now rendered in fight of the univerfe, at once to the rights of man, and to the philofopher who moft contributed, to extend the conquefts of liberty over the face of the whole earth?

Antiquity

Antiquity would have raised altars to that vast and mighty genius, who, for the advantage of human-kind, embracing earth and heaven in his ideas, could tame the rage of thunder and of despotism*. France enlightened and free, owes at least some testimony of remembrance and regret, to one of the greatest men, who ever served the cause of philosophy and liberty.

" I move you to decree, that the National Assembly shall wear mourning three days, for the late Benjamin Franklin."

Scarce was this funeral oration finished, when the tears which had interrupted it, were succeeded by the applause so well merited by the orator.

His motion was decreed with acclamations, and Monday 14th was fixed on for the first day of the mourning.

* Sut dompter la foudre et les tyrans.

It was then ordered, that the speech of Mirabeau should be printed, and that a letter should be written by the president to the congress of America, testifying the grief of the assembly for the death of Benjamin Franklin.

January 14, 1791.

The ecclesiastical committee had been enjoined by the assembly, to present it with an address upon the civil constitution of the clergy. Commissioners had been named for this purpose, when it was understood that Mirabeau had prepared a work on the same subject. The commissioners entreated that he would communicate it to them; and, after various observations concerning it, the address of Mirabeau was adopted by the committee.

The

The reading of this address proved an occasion, or a pretence, for much scandal. It is for men whose minds are free, exempt from prejudice, exempt from passion, to decide with calm reflection on the works of genius.

Plan of an Address to the French, upon the civil Constitution of the Clergy, adopted and presented by the Ecclesiastical Committee, to the National Assembly, on the 14th of January, 1791, and pronounced by M. de Mirabeau the Elder.

MEN OF FRANCE,

" At the moment when the National Assembly, is enjoining your new laws to pay attention to the priesthood, to the end that, in consequence of the reciprocal support

support experienced by all the inftitutions of the empire, your liberty may become unfhakeable, exertions are made to lead the confcience of the public into error. The voice of cenfure cries aloud from every quarter *, againft the civil conftitution of the clergy, decreed by your reprefentatives, as outraging the nature of the divine organization of the Chriftian church, and incompatible with the principles, eftablifhed and confecrated by ecclefiaftical antiquity.

" Might we not have broken the chains of our fervitude, without fhaking off the yoke of the faith?—No: liberty is far from prefcribing to us fo impracticable a facrifice. Behold, O fellow-citizens, behold the church of France, whofe foundations are interjoined and loft amidft thofe

---

* On denonce de toute part.

of

of the empire itself; observe how she rises into regeneration in conjunction with it; and how liberty, which, as well as our faith, descends from heaven, seems to present her as the companion of her eternity and her divinity! Observe how these two daughters of imperial Reason* unite, to develope and accomplish the perfection of your sublime nature, and to complete your double necessity, of existing with glory, and of existing everlastingly!

"We are reproached with having refused to decree explicitly, that the Catholic, Apostolic, and Roman religion, is *the religion of the nation.*

"With having altered, without the intervention of ecclesiastical authority, the

---

* I do not see how *Faith* can be called the daughter of *Reason*; matters of faith, says Mr. *Locke*, are above reason. W.

ancient demarkation of dioceses, and of having, by that measure, as well as in several other points of the civil organization of the clergy, given disturbance to episcopal power.

"Finally, with having abolished the ancient form of nominating the pastors, and transferred the determination to the suffrages of the people.

"Upon these three points turn all those accusations, of irreligion and persecution, by which attempts are made to dishonour the integrity, the wisdom, and the orthodoxy, of those who represent you. They are going to answer, less for their own justification, than with a view of prepossessing the real friends of religion, against the clamours of hypocrites who are enemies to the revolution. [*Here Mirabeau was applauded by a great part of the assembly.*]

"To

"To declare the Christian religion to be the *national* religion, would have been tantamount to blemishing the dearest and most essential characteristic of Christianity. In general, religion is not, nor can it be, a relation of civil society; it is a relation between man in his private capacity, and the infinite Being who created him. Should you comprehend their meaning, who would talk to you of *a national conscience?* Assuredly, religion is no more *national* than conscience: for a man is not really religious, merely because he belongs to some national religion; and, although there were but one religion known upon earth, and all humankind should agree to profess it, still were it true that each would feel a sincere sentiment of religion, only so far as each adhered firmly to his own; that is, only so far as he still held to that universal religion, although the human race were to abjure it. [*Here the applause recommenced.*]

"Therefore, in whatever light we view religion, to call it *national*, is bestowing on it an insignificant and ridiculous denomination.

"Were it as judge of its truth, or as judge of its aptitude to form good citizens, that a legislator would render a religion *constitutional?* But, in the first place, are there any *national* truths? In the second place, can it ever become conducive to the public good, that the consciences of men should be shackled by the law of the land? The law unites us to one another, only in those points where we touch. Now, man is tangible in his superficies only; in thought, and in conscience, he remains apart,

apart, and society leaves to him, in this respect, the absolute existence of nature. [*Fresh applause.*]

"Finally, there can be nothing *national* in an empire, but institutions established for the purpose of producing political effects, and religion being no more than the correspondence of the thought and the spiritual part of man, with the divine thought, with the universal spirit, it follows, that religion cannot, in this point of view, assume any civil or legal form. Christianity is principally excluded, by its own essence, from every system of local legislation. God created not that light, in order to lend forms and colours to the social organization of the French; but he hath placed it in the midst of the universe, to the end that it might serve as a point to rally

rally by, and as the centre of union to the whole human race. Why do they not as well blame us, for not having declared, that the sun is *the national luminary*, and that no other sun shall be recognized by law, for the regulation of our nights and days? [*Here the hall refounded with the applause of the assembly.*]

"Ministers of the gospel, you believe that Christianity is the profound and everlasting system of God; that it is the cause of the existence of a universe, and of a race called humankind; that it embraces all generations, and all times; that it is the bond of a society spread out through all the empires on the globe, *and which shall be re-assembled from the four quarters of the world*, to be exalted into the splendours of the unshakeable empire of eternity.

[*Here*

[*Here the right side of the hall laughed*, and the left applauded*] and, with these ideas thus vast, thus universal, thus superior to all human localities, you require, that, by a constitutional law of our young government, this christianity, so strong in majesty, and in antiquity, be declared the religion of the French ? You are they who are outraging the religion of our fathers; you are desirous, that, like those false religions, born of human ignorance, promoted by the tyrants of the earth, and confounded with political institutions, as an engine of oppression, it should be declared the religion of the law, and of the Cæsars!

" Undoubtedly, where an absurd belief hath given birth to a tyrannical go-

---

* Observe that the clergy sate on the right side of the hall. W.

vernment; where a wayward conſtitution is the offspring of a ſenſeleſs worſhip, religion muſt, indeed, form an eſſential part of the conſtitution.

" But Chriſtianity, weak and tottering at its birth, invoked neither the aid of laws, nor the adoption of governments *. Her miniſters would have rejected the idea of her exiſting *legally*, ſince it was neceſſary that God alone ſhould appear, in what was only his own work; and we ſhould, at this day, feel the want of the moſt ſtriking proof of its verity, had all thoſe, who, before our time, profeſſed

* Good.—On the contrary, it found a perſecutor in every ſovereign; in *primitive* chriſtianity, as delivered by Jeſus and his apoſtles, there was nothing that could flatter pride, or prove auxiliary to deſpotiſm. W.

that

that holy religion, discovered it in the legislation of empires.

" O strange inconsistency! what manner of men are they, who require of us, with a clamour, and a bitterness so unchristianlike, a decree for rendering Christianity *constitutional?* These are the very men who condemned the new constitution, who represented it as the subversion of all the laws of justice and of wisdom, who from every quarter exclaimed against it, as the instrument of perverseness, violence, and revenge. These are the very men who told us, that this constitution would prove the ruin of the state, and the disgrace of the French nation. O faithless men! wherefore would ye introduce a religion, which ye profess to cherish and adore, into a system of legislation which ye glory in decrying and detesting? Wherefore would ye unite, whatever is most august and most holy in the universe, with what ye consider as the most infamous monument of human malice? *What union*, Saint Paul would say to you, *can be established between justice and iniquity? And what can there be in common between Christ and Belial?* [Applause.]

"No, men of France, it is neither good faith nor sincere piety, which stirs up, amidst your representatives, these contests about religion; human passions are the cause, passions, which endeavour to hide themselves beneath an imposing mask, in order to cover with more impunity their dark and vile designs.

"Look back, survey religion in her cradle; there it is that you may form an idea of her true nature, and determine the mode

mode of exiftence, under which her divine founder, meant that fhe fhould reign over the univerfe. Chrift Jefus is the only one of all thofe fages, who have undertaken to inftruct men, and to render them good and happy, the only one who never beheld them in any political point of view, and who never, in any inftance, intermingled with his doctrine, principles that were connected with the legiflation of empires. Whatever be the influence of the Gofpel upon morality, neither Jefus Chrift, nor his difciples, ever gave men to underftand, that the evangelical difpenfation, was to form a part of the conftitutional code of every ftate. He no where enjoins thofe, whom he had chofen for the publifhers of his doctrine, to prefent it to the legiflators of the world, as containing new ideas upon the art of governing nations: "Go forth, and inftruct men, faying to them: Behold the kingdom of heaven is at hand; and into whatfoever city or village ye fhall enter, inquire who are they that be willing to give ear unto ye; and remain there as long as fhall be needful, for the teaching them what ye are to teach them; but if they refufe to hear ye, depart, and be in all things wife as ferpents and harmlefs as doves *." [*Applaufe.*]

"The gofpel, therefore, is, by the very nature of its inftitution, an economy wholly fpiritual, held out to humankind, inafmuch as we have a deftination beyond the boundaries of civil fociety, and confidered apart from all political re-

* The orator feems to have quoted this at random; but his purpofe was fully anfwered. W.

lations :

lations: it is propofed to man, as his fecond reafon, as a fupplement to his confcience*; and not to fociety, as a new object of legiflation. The gofpel, on its appearance in the world, required, that men fhould *receive* it, and that governments fhould permit it. And that is the exterior characteriftic which, at its origin, diftinguifhed it from every religion, which had tyrannized upon earth; and that likewife is what muft diftinguifh it, to the end of time, from every mode of worfhip which depends for its fupport, on its being incorporated into the conftitutions of empires.

" It is, therefore, a truth eftablifhed upon the very nature of things, upon found fenfe, and even on the effence of the gofpel difpenfation, that your reprefentatives,

---

* What an excellent phrafe!

sentatives, O men of France, neither ought, nor can decree the title of *national*, to the catholic, apostolic, and Roman religion.

" But, since Christianity is an economy wholly spiritual, above the reach of the power and inspection of men, wherefore have we taken upon us the right of altering, without spiritual intervention, the ancient demarkation of the dioceses?

" Assuredly, we might as well be asked wherefore we are Christians? wherefore we have assigned, upon the national treasury, the most solid portion of the revenues of the state, as a maintenance for the ministers of the gospel, and to defray the expences of public worship? [*Murmurs from the right.*]

" Next after the elements of the Christian constitution, its worship is the object of the free *acceptation* of men, and of the *toleration* of governments. It can be considered as no more than *tolerated*, as long as it is received and observed, by only a small number of the citizens of the state; but, when it is become the worship of the majority, it loses its appellation of *tolerated worship*; it is then *a worship received;* it is, in fact, *the religion of the public*, without being, of right, *the religion of the nation.* For a religion is not adopted by a nation, inasmuch as that nation is a power, but inasmuch as she is *a collection of men.*

" From this state of worship, its exercise having no correspondence with civil order, several consequences result.

" In the first place, ecclesiastical authority can distribute amongst the pastors, the spiritual direction of the faithful, according to such divisions or demarkations, as its wisdom shall prescribe; and the government, which is not connected by any point of contact with religious polity, hath nothing to oversee, nor to reform, in limitations which are not politically visible.

"Secondly, in this situation of worship, which, for so long a time, was the only one required by the ancient priesthood from the powers of the earth, the subsistence of the ministers, the construction and reparation of the temples, and every expence attending the ceremonial of religion, are charges foreign to the revenue; for that which does not belong to the institution politic, can have no relation to the jurisdiction of the public expenditure.

"Thirdly, but the moment that a Christian institution, adopted by the majority of the citizens of the empire, hath been

been *allowed* by the national power; the moment that this same power, undertaking all the charges of the temporal state of religion, and providing for all the wants of public worship and of its ministers, hath guarantied, upon the faith of the nation, and upon the funds of her revenue, the perpetuity and immutability of her acceptation of Christianity, from that moment, that religion hath received a civil and legal existence in the state, which is the highest honour that a nation can render, to the sanctity and majesty of the gospel; and from that moment likewise, it is to that national power, which hath bestowed a civil existence on the religious institution, that the right belongs of determining its civil organization, and of assigning to it its external and legal constitution. She may, and she ought to assume the government

ment of religion, as to the whole of that public character wherewith she hath impressed it, and in every point of contact where she hath established a relation between it and the social institution. She may, and she ought to challenge to herself, the regulation of worship, in whatever exterior circumstances she hath caused it to acquire, through the whole of that physical greatness of which she hath caused it to partake; throughout every relation, by which she hath connected it with the great machine of state; in fine, in every thing which appertains not to its spiritual, internal, and primitive constitution. It is, therefore, the right of the government, to regulate the demarkations of the dioceses, since they are the greatest public characteristic of religion, and the manifestation of its legal existence. The sacerdotal ministry is subordinate,

dinate, in the subdivision of the functions annexed to worship, to the same authority which prescribes limits to all the other public functions, and which determines all the bounds and circumscriptions in the empire.

" Let them tell us what they mean, by the intervention of spiritual authority, in a distribution wholly political. Does a nation, which, receiving into her bosom, and uniting to her government the Christian dispensation, so orders the system of all her administrations, that, wherever she finds men to govern, she appoints a prime pastor for their religious instruction, does such a nation arrogate a sacerdotal power? Does she plan any enterprize against the consciences of her flock, against the dogmata of the faith, against its sacraments,

sacraments, against its hierarchical relations and dependencies?

"But, we are told, the spiritual jurisdiction of the bishops hath changed with the ancient division of the dioceses; and it is highly necessary that the Roman pontiff intervene, for the purpose of granting to the bishops, powers adapted to the new constitution.

"Let those amongst our pastors, who have upright hearts, and minds capable of observation, soar above ideas and traditions, of a theology invented for the disfiguration of religion, and to render her subservient to the ambitious views of certain men, and they will find, that the founder of Christianity seems to have constituted its priesthood, with an eye to its future destiny; that is, that he framed it

in

in such a manner, as that it might lend itself to all the civil forms of those states, in which the Christian dispensation should be adopted, and exert itself in every direction, and according to every limitation, which the laws of empires should at any time assign to it.

"Was it by allotting to each of them a portion of authority, confined by territorial limits, that the author of our religion formed the apostolic institution? No: it was by conferring on each of them the plenitude of spiritual power, in such wise, that one of them, possessing the jurisdiction of all, was appointed the pastor of the whole human race. " Go," said our Saviour to them; " disperse your-
" selves over the face of the earth; preach
" the gospel to all mankind——I SEND
" YE, AS MY FATHER HATH SENT ME."

". If,

"If, then, at the time of their miſſion, the apoſtles had divided amongſt them, the inſtruction of the whole world, and, afterwards, the powers of earth had altered the limitations which they had voluntarily aſſigned to themſelves, would any of thoſe apoſtles have been diſquieted at finding, that his juriſdiction was no longer the ſame? Can it be ſuppoſed, that they would have reproached the public authority, with aſſuming the right of reſtraining or of extending that of the ſpiritualty? Can it be imagined, eſpecially, that they would have invoked the intervention of Saint Peter, in order to be reinſtated in the functions of the apoſtleſhip, by a new and extraordinary commiſſion?

" And wherefore ſhould they have had recourſe to that ſupreme head of the univerſal church? His primacy conſiſted not

in

in a greater fhare of fpiritual power, nor in a more eminent and more extenfive jurifdiction. He had received no particular miffion; he had not been appointed fhepherd of the Chriftian flock, by a fpecial inauguration, feparate from that of the other apoftles. Saint Peter became paftor by virtue of the fame words, which commiffioned all his colleagues to inftruct the world at large, and fanctify all mankind. [*Murmurs from the right.*] We fee, likewife, Saint Paul and the reft of the apoftles, eftablifhing priefts and bifhops, in the different countries whither they had carried the light of the gofpel, and appointing them fhepherds of the flocks, which they had acquired for Chriftianity: nor do we any where find, that they had called in the authority of

Saint Peter to their aid, nor that the new pastors had expected from him canonical institution.

"What? do the pontiffs of our religion no longer acknowledge, in their mission, the same character with which the apostles were invested? If it be true, that the Christian priesthood hath been instituted but once, for all ages ever afterwards, does not the apostolic power subsist at this day amongst the bishops, as successors of the apostles, in the universality of its primitive institution? Does not each of them, at the moment of his consecration, become what each apostle was, at the moment when he received his own, at the feet of the everlasting pastor of the church? And is he not SENT, as Jesus Christ was by his father? In fine, hath he not been invested

invested with a character*, suited to all places, to all men, and subsisting ever unaltered, amidst all the changes, all the crosses, and all the variations, which the demarkations of churches can experience?

" Be watchful of your conduct," saith Saint Paul to the bishops whom he had established in Asia; " be watchful of your " conduct, and of that of the flock, for " whose sake the Holy Spirit hath conse- " crated ye bishops, in giving to you the " government of the church of God, " which Jesus Christ hath founded by his " blood."——Weigh these words, and ask yourselves whether Saint Paul believed, in the *locality* of episcopal jurisdiction.

" The bishops, then, are essentially charged, with the direction of the univer-

* Une aptitude applicable, &c.—A bad mode of expression, surely.

sal church, as were the apostles: their mission is actual, immediate, and absolutely independant of all local limitation. The unction of episcopacy is sufficient for their institution, and they have no more occasion for the sanction of the Roman pontiff, than Saint Paul had for that of Saint Peter. [*Redoubled applause.*] The Roman pontiff is, as Saint Peter himself was, only the pastor singled out, to be the point of re-union to all the other pastors, to convene the judges of the faith, to be the depositary of the belief of all the churches, the conservator of the universal communion, the superintendant of the whole internal and spiritual administration of religion *.

" Now, all these relations established no distinction, nor any dependance really

* *Bravo!*

hierarchical,

hierarchical, between him and the bishops of the other churches; and the latter, when ascending their thrones, owe him nothing but the attestation of their union with the centre of the universal faith, and of their willingness to become pastors, in the spirit and in the sense of the Catholic belief, and to correspond with the holy see, as with the principal throne of that authority, which Jesus Christ hath bestowed upon his church [*].

" In ecclesiastical antiquity, they knew no other form for the installation of their pontiffs. *I profess*, said a bishop once in

---

[*] It should seem, then, that M. Mirabeau is of opinion, that the pope is only an œcumenical patriarch; and perhaps this is reducing that prelate to his just standard. Not but we of the Protestant communion, can very well dispense with any such officer. W.

a letter to pope Saint Damasus, *that I am united in communion to your holiness, that is to say, to the chair of Saint Peter. I know that the church hath been built upon that rock. Whoever eats the passover not in that house, is one of the profane. He who gathers not with you, is a spendthrift.* Here, then, is the precise description of that connection, which Jesus Christ established between Saint Peter and the other apostles, and the only rule of the correspondence, to be maintained between Rome and all the churches of Catholicism; and it is likewise the only rule which the National Assembly hath recommended to the chief pastors of the church of France.

"It is by recurring to this ancient and incorruptible source, of true ecclesiastical economy, that good minds will be convinced that the metropolitans receive,

by

by only *occupying* the fee set apart for that high station, all the powers which can be necessary to the exercise of such a function. Those boundaries purely territorial, which considerations of order and police, obliged government to prescribe to episcopal authority, are the only limitations ever acknowledged in the French empire.

" The metropolitan sees are themselves only establishments of police. The episcopate of the metropolitan, differs in nothing from that of his suffragans. His superiority over them, is not derived from any particular mission; but merely from the supremacy of the city, where his see hath been established. This sort of sacerdotal hierarchy, was entirely constructed upon the civil hierarchy, and the emperors, at their pleasure, erected the seat of those establishments.

" Far

"Far from having narrowed the episcopal authority, and lifted the simple priesthood to the level of episcopacy, in the dispositions which we have ordained with respect to its administration, we have rather restored to it that immensity which it enjoyed at its birth; we have destroyed all those limits, within which an ancient and thick cloud of prejudices and errors, had confined and concentred its exercise: unless it be called breaking the hierarchical gradation, which distinguishes the prime pastors from the subaltern clergy, to assign to the bishop of each church a council, and to enjoin that he shall not do any act of authority, *in what concerns the government of the diocese*, without having first deliberated with the presbytery of the diocese. As if that superiority, which the pontiff, by divine *law*, possesses over his clergy,

clergy, disencumbered * him from the duty imposed *by the law of nature*, on all men burthened with a vast and difficult charge, of invoking the assistance, and consulting the knowledge, of experience, of maturity, and of wisdom! As if, in this respect, as well as in so many others, the National Assembly had not re-established the usage of the first ages of the church! " Every thing there was done by council," says Fleury, " because there the sole object was, to establish the reign of reason, the reign of regularity, and of the will of God."—

" In each church, the bishop did nothing of importance, without consulting the priests, the deacons, and all his principal clergy; nay, he frequently consulted the whole people, when it was interested

* L'affranchissoit.

in the affair, as, for inftance, in the cafe of ordination*.

"But could and ought the fame power, which exclufively poffeffes the national legiflation, caufe the ancient form of appointing the paftors to difappear, and fubmit it to the election of the people?

"Yes, indubitably, that power poffeffed this right, if the difpofal of an office belongs effentially to thofe, who are at once the object and the end of fuch an office; and the priefthood of France owes alfo, on this confideration, the example of refpect and obedience.

"It is for men that a religion and a priefthood exift, and not for the Divinity, who cannot have occafion for them. "Every bifhop," fays Saint Paul, "elect-

---

* What impiety in all this!—Rank atheifm. W.

" ed from amongst men, is appointed for
" the service of men; it behoveth him to
" understand how to compassionate igno-
" rance, to condescend to the feeble, and
" to enlighten those that be in error."

" And, not only does the apostle here proclaim the right of the people, in ecclesiastical elections, as derived from the nature of things, but he likewise supports it, by particular considerations of order and of circumstances. The sacerdotal function is a ministry of humanity, of condescension, of charity, and of zeal. It is therefore that Saint Paul recommends, that it should be entrusted to men only, who are indued with a spirit truly sensible and paternal, to men only, who have been long exercised in beneficence, and well known to the public by their pacific inclinations, and by their habits of doing good.

good*. It is therefore, likewise, that he points out, as proper judges of their fitness for the pontifical functions, and to become pastors of the people, those who have been witnesses of their conduct, and the objects of their care †.

" And yet, because the National Assembly of France, commissioned to proclaim the sacred rights of the people, hath recalled it to the ecclesiastical elections; because the Assembly hath re-established the ancient form of these elections, and rescued from neglect, a mode of proceeding that was a source of glory to religion, in her vernal bloom of youth, lo! the ministers of that religion cry usurpation,

---

* More atheism.

† Was this better than a royal *congé d'elire* to a dean and chapter? that is, *the king gives his compliments to them, and insists that they shall elect for their bishop, a person whom, perhaps, they never before heard of.* W.

scandal, impiety; reproach, as a wicked attempt upon the imprescriptible authority of the clergy, the restoration of the right of election to the people, and dare to claim, as of necessity, the pretended concurrence of the pontiff of Rome!

"Formerly, when an immoral pope and an audacious despot fabricated, unknown to the church and to the empire, that profane and infamous contract, that *concordat* which was nothing more than the coalition of two usurpers, for the purpose of sharing between them the rights and the gold of France, the nation was seen, with the clergy at her head, opposing to this robbery the whole force of an unanimous resistance, demanding the restoration of the elections, and, with a persevering energy, laying claim to *the pragmatic sanction*, which alone, until then,

then, had constituted the common law of the kingdom. [*Applause.*]

"And it is this irreligious contract, this simoniacal convention, which, at the time when it was hatched, drew upon it all the anathemas of the sacerdotal order here; it is this criminal stipulation between avarice and ambition, this ignominious compact, which, through so many successive ages, was imprinting on the most hallowed functions the vile blemish of venality, this it is, which, at the present day, our prelates have the assurance to claim in the name of religion, in the face of the whole world, beside the cradle of liberty, in the very sanctuary of those laws, which are regenerating the altar and the empire*!

* What a paragraph!—I could almost snatch the crown of eloquence from the head of *Demosthenes*, and place it upon the brows of *Mirabeau*. W.

"But

" But, it is said, the choice of pastors, entrusted to the people, will prove nothing but the offspring of cabal.

" Amongst the most implacable detractors of the re-establishment of the elections, how many are there to whom we might make this dreadful answer? " Is
" it for you to borrow the language of
" piety, in order to condemn a law, that
" assigns you successors, worthy of the
" esteem and veneration of that people,
" which hath unceasingly besought Heaven
" to grant its children a pastor, who
" might be capable of comforting and edi-
" fying them? Is it for you to invoke
" religion, against the stability of the con-
" stitution, who ought to become its most
" steady supporters; you, who could not
" sustain, for a single instant, the sight of
" what ye are, if, on a sudden, rigid
" truth

" truth were to manifeſt, in full day, the
" dark and deſpicable intrigues which
" paved the way to your elevation*;
" [*Applauſe*]. you who are the creatures
" of the moſt wicked adminiſtration ; you
" who are the fruit of that formidable
" iniquity, which ſummoned to the moſt
" exalted ſituations in the prieſthood, thoſe
" who grovelled in ſloth and ignorance,
" and who unmercifully ſhut the doors of
" the ſanctuary, againſt the laborious
" and well-informed claſs of eccleſiaſtics ?"
[*Murmurs and ſymptoms of agitation, from the right.*]

M. *Gerard:* " Theſe are truths." [*A great part of the Aſſembly applauded.*]

Mirabeau in continuation: " How could theſe men, who make ſuch an often-

---

* *Bravo!*—More atheiſm.—I will worry them, as the Baſtard, in *King John*, worries the worthleſs Duke of Auſtria. W.

tatious

tatious show of zeal, to secure to the churches, a choice of pastors worthy of a name so sanctified, how could they so long sit silent, when they beheld the fate of religion, and the disposal of the august functions of the apostleship, abandoned to the nod of a minister, the slave of those intrigues which continually surround the throne? Opportunities of rising up against a sacrilegious traffic, presented themselves to the clergy, at conjunctures regularly returning; but how did the clergy act in those assemblies? Instead of seeking a remedy for this deplorable state of religion, and enlightening the wisdom of a pious and just prince, as to the impiety of leaving the care of providing pastors for the church of France, to the pitiless oppressors of the people, it frivolously lays down at the feet of the royal patron,

patron, a vain and pusillanimous tribute of adulation, and contributions, the burthen of which is imposed on that poor class, the assiduous and ever-resident labourers of the gospel. [*Fresh applause.*] What? is it not evident, that, had our prelates demanded another form of appointment to ecclesiastical offices, it would have been condemning too openly their anti-canonical creation, and avowing in the face of the nation, that they themselves were but intruders, whom it was necessary to turn out, and whose places ought to be occupied by others?

" But if, not daring to reproach, absolutely, the re-establishment of the elective form, for ecclesiastical employments, the prelates still insist, that the mode decreed by the constituting body, *is contrary to the ancient forms*, which always

allowed

allowed the priesthood the honours of superior influence, we shall ask them, whether they have discovered that that influence was founded, upon any precise law. of the evangelical constitution, and whether it was an effect of those rules by which the Redeemer, first organized the government of our religion? We shall ask them, of what kind were the first elections, which immediately followed the foundation of Christianity? A number of disciples was chosen, at the instigation of the apostles, seven men inspired by the Holy Ghost, and with wisdom, for the purpose of assisting them in the duties of the apostleship; these men received, from the apostles, the imposition of hands, and in that manner became the first deacons.

" And, in our days, when and in what manner did the clergy bear a part, in the task of distributing the diocesan and parochial offices? Episcopal fees were to be filled, and the king gave them away; rich abbeys were to be conferred, and the court conferred them; a great number of beneficed cures were at the disposal of lay patrons, and these lay patrons disposed of them*: a non-catholic, a Jew, by the mere acquisition of certain seigneuries, became the arbiter of the destiny of religion, and of the moral condition of a multitude of parishes; thus the great titles and the great offices of the church were parcelled out, without the participation, and even without the knowledge of the clergy; and what little right remained to it, of nominating to the obscure and subaltern benefices, served only to render its want of weight in the disposal of benefices, the more public and the more perceptible.

* A crying grievance in other kingdoms also. W.

"Undoubtedly, there was an age of the church, when the priesthood presided in assemblies, convened for the purpose of creating pastors, and when the people regulated its choice, according to the suffrages of the clergy. But why do not our prelates, instead of stopping at intermediate periods, when the primitive forms were already changed, search upwards to those very elections, so contiguous to the cradle of Christianity, when each city and each village had its pontiff, and when the people alone proclaimed and enthroned its spiritual pastor? For it is necessary to observe, that the associating the clergy to the elective assemblies, is dated from the diminution of the episcopal sees, that is, that it owes its origin to the difficulty of re-assembling, the multitude of those who belonged to a single church.

"At

"At this same period, when the priesthood was the soul of the convocations for the election of ministers, the poor and austere bishops bore the greatest part of the burthen of the religious ministry; the inferior priests were only their assistants; the bishops were the only persons who offered up the public sacrifice, who preached the word to the faithful, who catechised the children, who carried the alms of the church into the hiding-place of the unfortunate*, who visited the public asylums for age, indigence, and infirmity, who traversed with their blistered and venerable feet, the depths of the valley, and the sharp sum-

---

* *Bravo!*—More atheism.—It were a pleasant thing to see a modern Welch bishop perambulating the skirts of *Snowdon* or *Pen-maen-maûr*, peeping into the caverns of misery (for he could not *talk* to her), and scattering the half-crowns of the charitable judiciously. W.

mit of the mountain, for the purpose of dispensing knowledge and the comfort of the faith, amongst the innocent inhabitants of the fields and of the villages. Here are facts exactly parallel to that of the influence of bishops, over the election of spiritual pastors. Now are ye for transforming these *facts* into so many points of ecclesiastical *law*, and pronouncing that the conduct of prelates, who preach not the comforts of the gospel to their flock, and who travel in their sumptuous chariots, is contrary to the essential constitution of the church *? [*Repeated thunders of applause.*]

" The mode of election adopted by the National Assembly, is, then, the most perfect, since it is the most conformable

---

* This is, as *Pope* says,

" To goad the prelate slumbering in his stall." W.

to the proceedings in the time of the apostles, and nothing is so evangelical, and so pure, as what is derived from the high source of ecclesiastical antiquity.

" The criminal resistance made by a multitude of priests, to the laws of their country, their obstinate exertions, to revive the double despotism of the priesthood and the throne, have alienated from them the confidence of their fellow-citizens, and they have not been, in these days, summoned in any great number, to those bodies charged henceforward to proclaim the people's choice.

" But the time will arrive, when another generation of pastors, attaching themselves to the laws and to liberty, as to the source of their existence and their real grandeur, shall regain that high respect, which conferred so much authority

on

on the priesthood of the primitive church, and rendered its presence so dear to those majestic assemblies, where the hands of an innumerable people solemnly placed the sacred tiara, upon the head of the most humble and most wise.

" Then shall unquiet distrust and vexatious suspicion disappear; the confidence, the veneration, and the love of the poor, will open to the priests the gates of those assemblies, as to the most respectable conservators of the public mind, and of that patriotism which cannot be corrupted. It will be considered as an honour to pay a deference to their votes; for nothing is, in fact, more honourable for a nation, than to grant a great authority to those whom its own choice, could not summon to the great offices of religion, without being

being fully fenfible of the advantages of great talents, and of the merit of great virtues. Then fhall the priefthood and the empire, religion and the land, the fanctuary of the holy myfteries, and the temple of liberty and the laws, inftead of thwarting and juftling one another, according to the interefts by which men are divided, compofe only one grand fyftem of public happinefs; and France fhall teach the furrounding nations, that the gofpel and liberty are the infeparable bafes of all true legiflation, and the everlafting foundation of the moft perfect ftate of man.

"Behold the falutary and glorious epoch, which the National Affembly hath thought proper to prepare, which will be accelerated by the knowledge and the virtues of the priefthood, in concert with the
new

new laws, but which may be able also to subdue the prejudices, the passions, the resistance of that priesthood.

"Pastors and disciples of the gospel, who calumniate the principles of the legislators of your country, do ye know what ye are doing? You are comforting impiety for those insurmountable obstacles, which the law had opposed to the progress of its desolating system; and it is from you also that the enemies of Christianity expect, on this day, the abolition of all worship, and the extinction of every sentiment of religion. Imagine to yourselves the partisans of irreligion, calculating the gradations, by which the false zeal of the faith is conducting it to its ruin, and pronouncing in their circles the following discourse:

" Our representatives had replaced the
" edifice

"edifice of Christianity, upon its ancient
"base, and our measures for overturning
"it were for ever disconcerted. But what
"was to have given religion so great and
"so undisturbable * an existence, is now
"becoming the pledge of our triumph,
"and the signal of the downfal of the
"priesthood and its temples. Look at
"those prelates and those priests, who are
"exciting, through every province of the
"kingdom, the spirit of insurrection and
"rage; look at those treacherous protests,
"in which they threaten with the flames
"of hell such as receive the code of liber-
"ty; observe that affectation of bestow-
"ing on the regenerators of the empire
"the atrocious character of the ancient
"persecutors of the Christians; observe

* No such word in our dictionaries; but I don't care. W.

"those

" those priests and prelates unceasingly
" devising means, for getting possession
" of the public force, in order to em-
" ploy it against those, who have despoiled
" them of their ancient usurpations, in
" order to re-ascend the throne of their
" pride, in order to cause that gold which
" was their scandal and their shame, to
" flow back once again into their palaces;
[*Murmurs from the right, which are soon drowned in the applause from the left.*]
" see with what ardour they mislead the
" consciences, alarm the piety of the sim-
" ple, intimidate the weak, and how ea-
" gerly they exert themselves to make the
" people believe, that the revolution and
" religion can never subsist together.

" Now, the people will at last believe
" it; and, wavering in the alternative of
" being Christian or free, it will adopt that
" side

"side which will the less interfere, with
"its necessity for a respite from its ancient
"calamities. It will abjure its gospel; it
"will curse its pastors; it will no longer
"desire either to know or to adore, any
"other than the God who created nature
"and liberty. And then, whatever shall
"remind it of the God of the New Testa-
"ment, will become odious in its eyes;
"it will no longer desire to sacrifice but
"upon the altar of its country; it will
"look upon its ancient temples but as
"monuments, which can serve only to
"witness, how long it was the sport of
"imposture, and the victim of untruth:
[*Murmurs from several parts of the hall.*]
"it will, therefore, no longer endure,
"that the price of its sweat and blood,
"should be applied to the expences of a
"worship which it rejects, and that an
"immea-

" immeasurable portion of the public re-
" sources, should be assigned to a sacerdo-
" tal conspiracy. And behold how that
" religion, which hath resisted every
" shock of human controversy, was des-
" tined to that grave which its own mi-
" nisters were digging for it!"

"Tremble, men of France, left these calculations of infidelity, be not founded upon the most alarming probabilities. Should it not be believed, that all those who make it their study, to decry as wicked attempts upon the rights of religion, the proceedings of your representatives in the organization of the sacred ministry; should it not be believed, I say, that their object and that of the infidel is the same; that they look forward to the same catastrophe, and that they have resolved on the ruin of Christianity, provided

vided they may be revenged, and that they have left nothing untried for the recovery of their power, and for the purpose of replunging you in your former servility? [*Applause from the left; the Abbé Maury makes a bow to the assembly, and withdraws, followed by several ecclesiastics: others drop off, one by one.*] that is, that the sole difference which distinguishes, the irreligious doctrine of the ecclesiastical aristocracy, is, that the former doctrine pants after* the downfal of religion, only in order to secure more firmly, the triumph of the constitution and of liberty; and that the second is striding towards* the destruction of the faith, with no other hope than that of seeing it involve in its overthrow, the liberty and constitution of

* souhaite. † tend.

the

the empire. The one aspires to see the faith extinguished amongst us, only from a belief, that it is an obstacle to the complete deliverance of man; the other exposes the faith to the greatest dangers, with the design of ravishing from you those rights which you have re-acquired, and of enjoying once again your degradation and your misery. In fine, the one detests religion, only because she appears to sanction maxims favourable to tyranny, and the other voluntarily yields her up to all the hazard of a shock, from which she expects the return of tyranny, and the revival of all abuses. Thus the humane spirit which intermingles with the enterprizes of infidelity, against the gospel dispensation, softens, and in some measure induces us to pardon, the temerity and injustice which attend them. But what apology could be offered, for the mischiefs which our ecclesiastics are inflicting upon religion, with a view of replunging their fellow-citizens in woe, and of recovering an authority, the deprivation of which incenses all their passions, and is at variance with all their habitudes?

"O you who are at peace with Heaven and with your consciences; ye pastors, who have hitherto hesitated to affix the seal of your oath, to the new civil constitution of the clergy, from no other motive than a sincere dread of becoming accomplices in usurpation, call to mind those early times, when Christianity, reduced to concentrate all her majesty and all her treasures, in the dark and silent cavern, exulted with so pure joy, when tidings came to announce to her austere and reverend pontiffs, the repose of the sword of persecution; when the intelligence arrived, that a cruel reign was now no more, and that a wise and humane monarch had succeeded to the sceptre; when they could venture, from the deep caves where they had consecrated their altars, to go and comfort and confirm the meek piety of their disciples, and to emit, from under ground, some few sparks of that light divine, which they guarded as a precious deposit. Now, let us suppose, that one of those venerable men of Christ, issuing suddenly from the antique catacombs, where his ashes are confounded with the remains of so many martyrs, were to come this day, to contemplate in the midst of us, the glory with which religion here beholds herself surrounded, and were to discover, at one view, all those temples, those high towers, which shoot aloft

aloft into air the glittering emblems of Christianity, that cross evangelical, which soars from the highest point, of every department of this great and illustrious empire—what a spectacle for the eyes of one, who, from his birth-day to his grave, had never beheld religion, but in the caverns of the forest and the desert! What inexpressible delight! what transports! I think I hear him cry, as that stranger once did, on seeing the camp of the people of God: O Israel, how beauteous are thy tents! O Jacob, what order, what majesty in thy pavilions *!—

"Calm, then, O calm your apprehen-

---

* What painting, what imagery, what fervid and sublime eloquence! I know of nothing of the kind in *Cicero* superior to this paragraph. W.

fions, ye minifters of the God of peace and truth; blufh at your inflammatory exaggerations, and no longer furvey our work through the medium of your paffions. We are not afking you to fwear againft the law of your hearts; [*Several members from the right ſtart up and cry,* THIS IS RINGING THE ALARM BELL.] but we befeech you, in the name of that holy God, who is one day to judge us all, not to confound human opinions and fcholaftic traditions, with the facred and inviolable ordinances of the gofpel. If it be contrary to morality to act againft one's confcience, it is equally fo, to frame a confcience upon falfe and arbitrary principles. The obligation to *make* a confcience, is prior to the obligation to *follow* confcience. Public evils of the greateft magnitude, have been occafioned by men,

who

who imagined that they were obeying God, and securing their eternal salvation. [*Applause.*]

"And you, adorers of Christianity and of your country, men of France, faithful and generous, but high-spirited and grateful people, would you judge of the great changes which have just regenerated this vast empire? Contemplate the contrast between your former state, and the situation which you are to enjoy henceforward. What was France but a few months since? Sages invoked the name of liberty, and liberty was deaf to their prayers. Enlightened Christians asked, whither had fled the august religion of their fathers, and the true religion of the gospel was no where to be found. [*Murmurs from the right, applause from the left.*] We were a nation without country, a people

without

without government, and a church without character and discipline."

M. *Camus* exclaims: " One cannot listen to this; I move that the assembly adjourn, that this business be referred to the ecclesiastical committee, and that nothing further be done here this day."

The members from the right crowd disorderly through the hall; some move towards the table, others towards the tribune: some members too from the left quit their seats. For several minutes the assembly experiences a violent agitation.— Different persons attempt to speak—A general murmur drowns their voices.

M. *Régnault de Saint-Jean-d'Angely* was of opinion, that the matter should be referred to the ecclesiastical committee, in order to undergo a new revision.

MIRABEAU.

"It is not merely the revision which should be ordered, but the utter disfiguration of the address, against which this outcry hath been raised. One fact I ought to mention, which is, that since the second and last reading, which it underwent in the ecclesiastical committee, I have not altered a single word of my address, no, not an iota. For my own personal justification, I demand that the address be stated, as it actually is at this moment. It ought to be thoroughly known; there should not be room even to suspect an alteration; it contains not one line, not a single expression, for which

which I will not anfwer, on my honour, and with my head*."

Mirabeau depofits his addrefs upon the table, and caufes the fecretaries to fign it.

The referring it to a committee was decreed by a great majority.

Mirabeau in continuation: " There was nothing regular and ftable amongft us, but the flagrancy of every vice, but the fcandal of all injuftice, but the public contempt of Heaven and of men, but the utter extinction of the laft principles of religion and of morality. What a country! where every thing was at the abfolute difpofal of certain men without reftraint, without honour, without know-

---

* Here I have been obliged to reverfe the original, in two particulars.—" Pas une expreffion, pas 'une ligne, dont je ne repond fur ma tête, et fur mon honneur."—He fhould have kept his *head* for the laft ftake. W.

ledge, and in comparison to whom, God and the human race were accounted nothing! And what a revolution that, which, on a sudden, causes such disorder to be succeeded by a spectacle, where every thing is placed and ordered according to the ancient wish of nature, and where no longer reigns any dissonance, but that occasioned by the powerless rage, of certain hearts incapable of rising to the loftiness of patriotic sentiments, and formed to continue grovelling in the meanness of their selfish passions!

" Men of France, you are the victors of your liberty, you have re-produced it in the bosom of this vast empire, by the grand exertions of your courage; it behoves you now to preserve it, by your moderation and your wisdom. Breathe around you the spirit of patience and of reason;

reason; pour the balm of fraternal consolation into the hearts of those of your fellow-citizens, from whom the revolution hath exacted mournful sacrifices; and never forget that, if the regeneration of empires can be no otherwise accomplished than by the explosion of the people's force, neither can it be otherwise preserved, than by the recollection of the virtues of peace. Think that the repose and silence, of a nation victorious over so many efforts and conspiracies, directed against her liberty and happiness*, are also the most formidable species of resistance, to that tyranny which would endeavour to overthrow her ramparts; and that nothing more effectually disconcerts the designs of the malignant, than the tranquillity of noble hearts."

* Transposed—son bonheur, et sa liberté.

JANU-

January 28, 1791.

Speech on the Measures relative to the external Defence of the State.

An almost universal alarm had been spread, concerning the external security of the state, on account of the evident dispositions of the powers of Europe, with regard to France.

The military and diplomatic committees, and the committee of research, united in considering of means of defence.

M. *Lameth* presented to the assembly measures applicable to all times, and which were calculated to form a general system of the military force of France; the same member then proposed the plan of a decree.

MIRABEAU.

"The diplomatic committee, in conjunction with that of war and that of researches, hath commissioned me to call your attention to an object, important from its being connected with the general tranquillity, namely, those rumours of war, those public alarms, which suspicion credits, and which zeal also is disseminating; those dangers, whatever they be, which it behoves us to appreciate by their reality, not by the impotent wish of those who are enemies to this country; those measures, in fine, which are compatible at once with our dignity and our interest: measures which policy alone makes it our duty to adopt, and which may reconcile what is due to credulity, to ignorance, and to prudence.

"To

"To an immenſe people, ſtill agitated by the movements of a great revolution; to new citizens, whom the firſt dawn of patriotiſm is uniting in the ſame notions, through every quarter of the empire, who, bound by the ſame oaths, ſentinels for one another, communicate rapidly all their hopes and all their fears, the bare exiſtence of alarms is perilous; and when meaſures of mere precaution, are adequate to quiet them, the inaction of the repreſentatives of a brave people were a crime.

"If the queſtion were only to inſpirit the men of France, we might ſay to them: Be more confident in yourſelves, and in the intereſts of your neighbours. Which country is the cauſe of your apprehenſions? The court of Turin will not ſacrifice a uſeful alliance, to reſentments, domeſtic or foreign. She will never disjoin her

her politics from her position; and the projects of cabal will be discomfited by her wisdom.

" Switzerland, that land of freedom, Switzerland faithful to treaties, and almost French, will furnish neither arms nor soldiers to that despotism which she hath crushed; she would be ashamed to protect conspirators, to countenance rebels.

" Leopold hath been a legislator, and his laws likewise had their detractors and their enemies. If he be possessed of numerous armies, he hath vast frontiers to defend. Were war his passion, although his reign hath commenced with peace, it is not towards the south, that true policy would allow him to march his legions. Would he teach provinces still fluctuating between an essay upon liberty, in which they have been disappointed, and the prudence

dence of a submission, which will last only as long as it shall be supportable, how men, who, at home, have abased the pride of tyranny, can resist the invasive arm of a conqueror?

"Are you afraid of a few princes of Germany, who affect to think that the government of a sovereign nation, should be arrested in the execution of her laws, out of respect for some privileged portions of their territories? But were their interests better asserted, by battles than by negotiations? and would they risk the indemnification which your justice hath awarded to them? That, in barbarous ages, the feudal system armed castles against castles, may be readily conceived; but that nations should go to war, for the purpose of continuing a few villages in slavery, is what even they who throw

out

but such threats, never entertained a thought of. Believe rather, that if the progress of our revolution gives disquiet to our neighbours, that apprehension is a pledge, that they will not come to trouble us with dangerous provocations.

"Are some French refugees, some soldiers privately enlisted, the origin of your fears? But hath not the hatred of such enemies been evaporating, to this day, in unavailing menaces? Where are their allies? What nation of any consequence, will undertake the task of revenging them, will supply them with arms and with subsidies, will waste, for their sakes, the produce of her taxes, and the blood of her citizens?

" Will it be England?

" With respect to the other powers of Europe, it is sufficient to penetrate the probable views of cabinets; but when Great-Britain is in queſtion, we muſt liſten alſo to the voice of the nation. What have we to hope or to fear, from the Engliſh miniſtry? To lay now the grand foundations, of an eternal brotherhood between their nation and ours, were a profound ſtroke of politics, as virtuous as it is rare; to watch the courſe of events, to put himſelf in a condition to act a conſpicuous part, and perhaps to diſturb Europe, in order to avoid remaining idle, were the trade of an intriguer, who worries fame for a day's triumph*, ſince he hath not credit to live by a beneficent adminiſtration. What? will the Engliſh miniſter, placed between theſe two careers, enter on that which will produce ad-

---

* Fatigue la renommée un jour.

vantage without splendour, or on that which will be attended either with splendour or with calamity? I cannot tell, gentlemen; but this I know, that it were not prudent in a nation to depend upon political virtues and exceptions. I shall not, in this respect, seduce you into too great a security; but I shall not hold my tongue, at a juncture when some amongst us are defaming the English nation, in consequence of that pamphlet of a member of the House of Commons, whom every admirer of great talents hath been afflicted at perceiving, amongst the superstitious calumniators of human reason; I shall not bury in silence what I have derived from the most authentic sources, namely, that the English nation rejoiced, when we proclaimed the great charter of humanity, discovered amongst the ruins of the Bastille; I shall

not conceal, that, if some of our decrees have shocked the episcopal or political prejudices of the English, those very English have taken a pleasure in applauding our liberty, because they are well aware, that all free nations, form a league of mutual security against tyrants; neither shall I omit to mention, that, from the midst of that nation so respectable at home, a terrible voice would issue, against ministers who should dare to undertake a savage crusade, for the destruction of our new constitution; yes, from the bosom of that classic land of liberty, there would issue a volcano, ready to swallow up the guilty faction, which should have attempted to try on us the infernal art of enslaving nations, and of loading them again with the chains which they have broken. The
ministry

ministry would not despise this public sentiment, which creates less noise in England, but which is as strong, and more steady, than amongst us*. It is not, then, an open war that I am inclined to fear: the embarrassed state of their finances, the ability of their ministers, the generosity of the nation, the enlightened men whom she possesses in such multitudes, assure me that no direct attempts will be made against us; but dark manœuvres, secret practices to excite disunion, to balance parties, to play them off one against the other, to oppose the rapid progress of our prosperity, are what we have to fear from certain malignant politicians. They might

* Hath he not well contrasted the solid taciturnity of the English character, with the restless sensibility of the French? W.

hope, by favouring discord, by prolonging our political warfare, by giving hopes to the discontented, by irrationally permitting one of our ex-ministers, to flatter those malcontents with vague encouragement, by letting loose upon us an outrageous writer, easily to be disowned, because he belongs to the opposition, they might hope, I say, to see us fall by degrees, into the state of being equally disgusted with despotism and liberty, to see us despair of ourselves, to see us pine away slowly, to see us extinguished by a political consumption; and then, feeling no more anxiety as to an influence on our liberty, they would not have to dread that extremity so truly insupportable to ministers, of sitting tranquil in the midst of Europe *,

of

---

* I confess, I do not altogether agree here with M. *Mirabeau*. Ministers are not always to sit idle spectators

of cultivating at home the peculiar means of their own happiness, and of renouncing that proud bustle, those mighty strokes of state, which impose upon the world, because few are able to judge of them, in order to apply themselves plainly to the care of governing, of administering, of rendering the people happy; cares which delight them not, because the nation at large can decide upon their value, and room is no longer left for imposition *. Such might be the insidious policy of the cabinet, without the participation, and even without the knowledge of the people of England; but such policy is so base, that it

spectators of what is doing in Europe;—*the balance of power* is not such a chimera, as some men seem to imagine. W.

* Or rather *state quackery*;—la charlatanerie.— *Bravo!*

is impossible to impute it to any except an enemy to humanity, so narrow, that it is adapted to men of only the most vulgar minds, and so well known, that, in our days, it is little to be dreaded.

" Men of France, extend, then, your views beyond your frontiers; you will there see only neighbours, who, like you, have need of peace, and not of enemies; you will there find men, who, in case of unjust war, can no longer be led to battle, with the same facility as formerly: citizens, who, less free than ourselves, consider, in secret, the success of our revolution, as an object of hope in which they themselves are interested. Next, traverse with your eyes the extent of this great empire, and, if you be possessed with the suspicion of zeal, pay likewise some respect to that force which is peculiar to you. You are
told,

told, that you have no army, while all your citizens are so many soldiers; that you have no longer any treasure, when, at the slightest hint of danger, the fortunes of individuals would become the fortune of the state; that a war might give a shock to your new constitution, as if the tents of a camp would not as soon become an asylum, for the legislators of a people, who enacted its first laws in the Champ-de-Mars. Eh! what senseless tyrant would expose himself, to conquer what he could not preserve? When the majority of a nation is resolved to continue free, is there any force that can hinder her from being so?

" Where, then, is the source of that anxiety, which, propagating itself through the realm, hath there called forth not only the energy and pride of patriotism, but likewise likewife its impatience? Hath not zeal been exaggerating our danger? for there is an ambition to ferve one's country, which may deceive the intentions of the beft citizen, which may induce him to create opportunities of being more powerful, in order to be at the fame time more ufeful; which may lead him to magnify his fears, becaufe he thinks himfelf a proper perfon to allay them; in fine, which may urge him to impart the firft impulfe, towards an object to which his talents decoy him*, and which, from that fole circumftance, occafions him to forget his difcretion.†

"Perhaps

---

* Entraîné par fon talent.

† Eminently prudent ftatefman, yourfelf, who laboured to fortify your country, not only againft the encroachments of royalty, and the infidioufnefs of faction,

" Perhaps, too, weary of their inability to disturb the kingdom, the enemies of the revolution have mistaken their wishes for their hopes, their hopes for realities, their menaces for an attack; and, consoling themselves with reveries of vengeance, have breathed inquietude amongst a people, more capable of judging of their audacity than of their means.

" Perhaps also, some men of faction, who are looking for some chance of executing, under the noble name of liberty, certain schemes concealed from us, have hoped to find them in the midst of a great popular agitation; and this contest of intrigue and ambition, against the generous

faction, but even against the well-meant, but mischievous endeavours of patriots, whose judgments are led astray by vanity. W.

credulity

credulity of patriotism, is undoubtedly a species of war.

"In fine, ought we not to confider, as one of the caufes of the public alarm, that extravagant diftruft, which fo long hath difquieted every bofom, which retards the moment of peace, embitters our diftreffes, and becomes a fource of anarchy, in ceafing to be of ufe to liberty? We are in dread of foes without, and forget the foe who is ravaging the very bowels of the kingdom. Almoft every where, the public functionaries, elected by the people, are at their refpective pofts; its rights, then, are exercifed; it remains for it to fulfil its duties. While overfeeing its commiffioners, let it honour them with its confidence, and let the turbulent force of the many, yield to the calmer power of law.

Then,

Then, till the signal of danger be given by the public functionary, the citizen shall say: *My interests are taken care of;* for that is not true liberty, which lives in idle terrors; she respects herself too much, to look on any thing as formidable *.

" However, gentlemen, if the fears of the public be extravagant, they are not therefore devoid of foundation. It is but too true, that there have been preparations, for an irruption of armed conspirators by the frontiers of Savoy; that some men have been enlisted in Switzerland, for the French mal-contents; that attempts have been made for

* *Cicero* complains, that even the periods of *Demosthenes* did not satisfy his ear. May I venture to observe, that *Mirabeau*, so happy in the construction of his sentences, fills the ear better than *Demosthenes*, without falling into the redundancy of *Cicero?* W.

clandestinely introducing arms into the kingdom; that measures have been taken, and still are taking, to draw certain princes of Germany into a quarrel which does not concern them, and to deceive them with regard to their true interests; in fine, that the refugees of France have agents, in several of the northern courts, for the purpose of decrying our constitution, the advantages of which sufficiently avenge it of their outrages.

" All these circumstances united, when compared with the force of a great people, were, perhaps, undeserving of our attention. But we ought also to take into the account, the uncertainty even of prudence, the winding ways of false policy, and the obscurity which ever partially envelopes what is to come. In fine, does not wisdom direct us, to rouse the courage

rage of even those, who have suffered themselves to be alarmed without reason?

" It is after having weighed every one of these considerations, that your committees move you, gentlemen, to adopt the following proposals:

" To organize, for the state of war, the national guards, and the auxiliaries; your military committee will point out to you the means:

" To determine what pensions shall be allowed to the several agents of the executive power, employed in foreign courts, in case of the appointment of successors.

" In fine, to place upon a war footing, that division of your army, which shall be cantoned in those parts of the kingdom, with respect to which any fears have been entertained.

" Every one hath, for this long time,

acknow-

acknowledged, and the minister for foreign affairs hath, more than once, represented to the diplomatic committee, the necessity of employing henceforward, in our transactions with foreign states, men who will not bring into question the power of the French nation, by doubting of our success; men who are not, in some measure, strangers to the new language of which they ought to be the organs, and who, whether it be that they are ignorant of the regeneration of their country, or that ancient prejudices combat with their duty, or that the inveterate habit of being the hirelings of despotism *, does not suffer them to reach the loftiness of a system of liberty, would be no more than agents of the minister, or

* De servir le despotisme.

confidents

confidents of the aristocracy, and not the representatives of a magnanimous people.

"But here it becomes necessary, it is at all times necessary, to reconcile interest with justice, and prudence with humanity. A long exercise of public functions, in a career where the fortune of an individual is often risked, entitles him to an honourable provision; and your dignity will not suffer you to refuse that recompense, even though you should not owe it to his services.

"With respect to the detaching a part of your military force, it is a debt that you must pay to opinion, which demands it. It is in order to prevent, at every the slightest danger, the necessity of summoning the entire nation into arms, from that labour which alone forms a nation, that you must detach a portion of the public force, and embolden the citizen by the forecaft of the law. Be under no apprehenfion, that our neighbours confider the re-affembling of the troops, either as a menace, or as an event capable of infpiring them with fufpicion. Our policy is frank and free, and we glory in it; but as long as the conduct of other kingdoms fhall be enveloped in clouds, who can blame us for taking precautions adapted to maintain tranquillity? No, an unjuft war can never become the crime of a people, that was the firft to engrave upon the table of its laws,' its utter renunciation of conqueft. Invafion is not to be apprehended from thofe, who defire rather to efface the limits of every empire, in order to form all mankind into one fraternal family, who would fain build an altar to peace, upon a mount compofed of all thofe inftruments of deftruction, with which Europe is covered and defiled, and preferve, for the fole purpofe of overawing tyrants, thofe weapons which have been hallowed by the noble prize of liberty *."

After this follows the decree relative to the penfions already mentioned, and to the feveral complements of troops neceffary for the protection of the kingdom.

PRESIDENTSHIP OF MIRABEAU.

February 1, 1791.

Mirabeau prefident!—We will not fay that it was an honour due to him; but we will be bold to fay, that the National Affembly conferred an honour on itfelf,

* Bravo!

in calling him to that office. Should any, who are strangers to the tactics, which, for so long a time, kept Mirabeau from the chair, be surprised at the boldness of our opinion, we would answer them thus: Either you look upon the presidentship as the premium of services rendered to the revolution, or you think that every member should be summoned to it indifferently. In the first case, we have no occasion to prove, that the name of Mirabeau ought to have been found at the head of the list of members, who have been elevated to the chair; in the second case, we also should experience some astonishment, that Mirabeau had been only the forty-fourth president.

February 10, 1791.

A deputation from the Quakers is introduced at the bar.

This sect of persecuted Christians, which still adheres to the ancient simplicity of the gospel, a sect, the religious principles of which inspire an abhorrence of shedding blood, a sect, in fine, with which a *yes* or a *no* is equivalent to an oath, was worthy of a maternal reception from the National Assembly.

MIRABEAU

TO THE DEPUTATION.

" The Quakers, who have fled from persecutors and tyrants, could not but address themselves with confidence to legislators, who have been the first to digest the rights

rights of man into laws; and to France regenerated, France in the bofom of peace, an inviolable refpect for which fhe will continually recommend, and which fhe wifhes to all other nations, in order to become likewife a happy Penfylvania. As a fyftem of philanthropy, your principles are entitled to our admiration; they remind us, that the cradle of each fociety, was a family united by its manners, by its affections, and by its wants. Indubitably, the moft fublime inftitutions would be thofe, which, effecting a fecond creation of humankind, fhould approximate to that prime and virtuous origin.

" An enquiry into your principles, confidered as opinions, concerns not this affembly. We have made our declaration. The effufions of the foul, the tranfports of the mind, are a property which none
will

will confent to enjoy in common; that facred domain exalts man into a hierarchy, more elevated than civil fociety. As a citizen, he adopts a form of government; as a thinking being, he hath no country but the univerfe. Confidered as a religious principle, your doctrine fhall not become the object of our debates; the connection of each individual with him who dwells on high, is independant of all political inftitutions; between God and the heart of man, what government fhall dare to interpofe? Confidered as civil maxims, your claims muft be fubmitted to the difcuffion of the legiflative body. It will examine, whether the form which you obferve, in certifying births and marriages, give fufficient authenticity to that filiation of the human fpecies, which, independently of good morals, the diftinctions of property render indispensable. It will inquire, whether an affirmation, the falsity of which would be subject to the punishment appointed for false witnesses and perjurers, were not really a false oath.

" Estimable citizens, you deceive yourselves; you have already taken that civic oath, which every man who deserves freedom, hath considered rather as an act of rejoicing, than as a duty. You have not taken God to witness, but you have attested your conscience, and is not an unspotted conscience likewise a cloudless Heaven? Is not that part of man an emanation of the Divinity? You say, moreover, that an article of your religion, prohibits you to carry arms, and to kill, under any pretence whatever. Undoubtedly, it must be a beauteous principle of philosophy, which enjoins, in some sort, such a tenet to human nature. But reflect, whether the defence of one's-self, and of one's fellow-creatures, be not likewise a religious duty. Would you, then, have bowed the neck to tyranny? Since we have acquired liberty for you and for ourselves, on what grounds should you refuse to preserve it? Had your brethren of Pensylvania been less remote from the savages, would they have suffered their wives, their children, and their old men to be massacred, rather than make any exertion to repel the fierce invader; and are not stupid tyrants, and ferocious conquerors, equally savage as the roving Indian of America?

" The assembly will, in its wisdom, discuss all your demands; and whenever I meet a Quaker, I will say to him: Friend,

Friend, if thou haft a right to be free, thou haft a right to hinder any from making thee a flave. Since thou loveft thy fellow-creature, do not leave him to be butchered by the hand of defpotifm; it were as if thou thyfelf wert his deftroyer. Thou defireft peace; but it is weaknefs which calleth for war; univerfal refiftance were univerfal peace.—The affembly inviteth ye to be prefent at its deliberations."

Many and reiterated teftimonies of applaufe had frequently interrupted this refponfe; at its conclufion they recommenced with double vigour.

MARCH 22, 23, 24, and 25, 1791.

These four days were devoted, for the most part, to the debates upon the plan of a law respecting the regency.

This plan gave rise to several questions. We shall confine ourselves to reporting those, which contained the greatest number of difficulties, and upon which Mirabeau declared his opinion.

First question. Shall the regency be hereditary or elective?

Second question. In case the minor king should have no kindred, possessed of all the requisite qualifications, shall the election be made by an electoral body, or shall the regent be appointed by the legislature *?

Third

* I apprehend that they have here used the word *legislature* improperly; for, until a regent be elected, there

Third question. At what age shall the minor king be impowered to take his seat in the council?

Messieurs Mirabeau, Cazalés, and the Abbé Maury, were for adjourning.

MIRABEAU.

" If I am inclined to an adjournment, it is not that I think with M. Cazalés, that the question of the regency involves a number of others, which will call for ample discussion. It is true, that, not having been able to meditate upon this plan, as I was extremely indisposed, [*Murmurs*] I have not yet made up my

---

there can be no complete legislature.—*Mirabeau*, in a former speech, was very angry with M. *Barnave* for terming the legislative body, the legislative *power*; the king being intitled to a *veto*. W.

mind

mind upon it. [*Murmurs again*] Since you seem so desirous of it, I must tell you, that you yourselves also have not sufficiently considered it. My opinion was, that a plan of a law, containing several pages, and which you have not been able to compare with the foundations, might appear to an assembly so wise as this is, to be worthy of not being decided on at this moment. I have no objection to your proceeding to a division, if I am mistaken in this point, namely, that you cannot comprehend in an instant, a plan amounting to eight pages; [*More murmurs.*] I have no objection to my being prevented from making an observation, with respect to the first article. I differ from M. Cazalés. He is wrong in supposing, that we may declare it impossible for the regent, in any sense, to be charged with the guardianship of the royal minor; the regent being the instrument of the kingly office, and therefore bound to a universal superintendancy. The plan of the committee is more conformable to the principles. The complexion which M. Cazalés seems desirous of giving to it, appears to me less rational, and also ill expressed. With regard to the various articles contained in the plan, there are some considerable chasms which ought to be filled up. But my first conceptions are never of much value, in my own eyes; judge what they are likely to prove in the opinion of others."

The assembly decreed, that the discussion should take place on that very day: accordingly, the battle began.

M. Barnave thought with the committee, that the regency being subsidiary to the kingly office, nay, an intermediate royalty,

royalty, it ought to be established upon the very same principles, and, therefore, that the regency should have the same unity as the royalty.

The opinion of the Abbé Maury, tending to render the regency elective, must have surprised the left side of the hall.

MIRABEAU.

"It appears to me, that, from the clashing of opinions, there is one question which ought to be determined, as a preliminary to all further debate. M. Barnave wishes the regency to be hereditary, like the royalty. The Abbé Maury is for having it elective. I confess, that I have been astonished, at seeing the same arguments applied, without any examination, to the heirship of the regency, which determined

mined you to decree that the monarchy should be hereditary. Why hath the monarchy been declared hereditary, notwithstanding the incommensurable disadvantages of such a form? It was because the disadvantages attending an elective monarchy, were, perhaps, still greater*, and more formidable to public tranquillity and social order. But if these disadvantages are not to be found, in the circumscribed, the very circumscribed election † of a regent, why endeavour to avoid them, by introducing those of heirship? Why accept a regent from the hands of

---

* It is the opinion of Lord *Bolingbroke*, that many successive reigns of virtuous princes, could not compensate for the mischiefs occasioned by one election. W.

† L'élection très-circonscrite.—May not the repetition of the adjective produce a beauty?

chance?

chance? This grand question, whether the regency shall be hereditary or elective, ought, therefore, to be previously decided. It is my wish that the discussion be reduced to this point. [*Applause.*] I would next ask leave to speak, for the purpose of enquiring, whether the regency should be elective, and whether there be good reasons for accepting a regent from the hand of chance.

M. Barnave combated with success, the opinion which Mirabeau had rather intimated than pronounced. It was his wish, that, in the case, which must very rarely happen, of an election, for want of a regent by right of birth, the election should be in the legislature, and not in an electoral body, as was proposed by the committee. M. Barnave was struck with the dangerous expedient, of assembling and placing eight hundred electors, beside the legiflative body.

MIRABEAU.

"Since no oppofition is made to the ftating the preliminary queftions, I mean not to anticipate the decifion, for I have not yet formed my opinion; and it is not after having complained, of the hafte fhewn by the affembly to difcufs a matter of this nature; it is not after having invoked the illumination of debate, that it would prove agreeable to me to enter into one. [*Murmurs from feveral quarters.*] I fhall anfwer, like a man who is as little likely to be ftunned by applaufe as by murmurs, that I have a refpect for forcible objections, and that I even fet fome value upon fpecious ones, fince they compel one to look again into one's felf, and to meditate;

meditate; but I shall make a few observations, upon what hath been hazarded by the member who spoke last, and who seemed desirous of prejudging the question. And first, as to the fact alleged by that gentleman, I answer, that it does not exist, and that the assembly having as yet come to no resolution, with respect to the inviolability of the regent, with respect to the identity of the functions, the rights, and the duties, assigned to the regency and to the royalty, it cannot be said, that the identity of the regency and the royalty, obliges us to render the former hereditary, like the latter. As to what regards the crisis, of which so terrifying a picture hath been drawn, in the case of an election, I answer, that it is what all regencies, all minorities are exposed to. The vacancy of the throne, the minority of a prince, is at all times a grand crisis in political affairs; but then, it is unavoidable, and is but little to be feared, in a well-constituted government.

"I come now to the third objection; and I declare, that it seems to me to deserve to be sifted in every particular, because it is rational, and, in some points of view, even weighty. Unquestionably, an elective regent would win more favour than one hereditary, because the choice resulting from reflection and from confidence, confers, and ought to confer more credit than that of chance. This objection, then, should be examined; but it derives no weight, from the examples just quoted by the member who spoke before me. In the moral and political shocks which we have experienced, for these two years past, two, three, or ten men, had they formed

the

the projects which have been matter of suppofition, would, in cafe of fuccefs, have only arrived a little fooner, and with a little more certainty, at the gallows.—Since mention hath been made of Cromwell, I fhall relate a witticifm of that ufurper, who fo well underftood both men and things, fince he had formed fo ftrong an intereft, and had given to that intereft fo powerful a direction. He was paffing along, attended by Lambert * his trufty companion; acclamations and *bravo* refounded from every fide. Lambert was delighted to enthufiafm at this reception. Cromwell, that great fearcher of the human heart, faid, in order to humble his friend's vanity: *They would huzza us much more, if we were mounting the fcaffold.*

---

* Mirabeau calls him *Lambel*. W.

"Gentlemen, do not imagine, that when a constitution is made, a great, and, especially, a durable interest, can be derived from a momentary crisis; and be assured, that in an affair of this nature, as in every other, one reaps nothing different from what one hath sown. While I was speaking, and expressing my first ideas upon the regency, I heard several say, with that agreeable decisiveness*, to which my ears have been long accustomed: *This is absurd, this is extravagant, this is not fit to be mentioned.* For my part, I declare that I know, in this assembly, some very worthy citizens, some very enlightened minds, who entertain great doubts upon the question, and who are preparing to support the plan of an elec-

* Indubitabilité.—Our language does not enable me to imitate this word. W.

tive

tive regency. I thence infer, that the question ought to be stated, so as to be capable of undergoing the necessary discussion, and that, when any thing is proposed, of what nature soever it be, before we cry out: *This is absurd, this is extravagant, this is not fit to be mentioned*, it behoves us to reflect well upon it, a mode of conduct which, be the state of the question what it may, never proves of any disservice."

The discussion of the question, whether the regency should be elective or hereditary, now assumes a more determinate character. We lament our not having it in our power to analyse the speeches of orators, who have developed principles on the opposite side.

M. *Pethion* was against the project of

the committee, as to what concerned the hereditary regency.

MIRABEAU.

"I said, yesterday, in this assembly, that my opinion upon the present question was not yet formed; nevertheless, the evening papers have eagerly set forth, that I had preached an elective regency; but who cares for the evening papers? let us proceed to the question.

"Shall the regency be hereditary or elective, or rather (for a regent does not succeed any thing, and accordingly the expression, *hereditary regency*, is improper) shall the regency be fixed invariably, or shall we only determine the mode in which the regency should be formed? Such

Such is the true quèftion, in which I have perceived, as well as on feveral other occafions, that many miftake their own horizon for the boundaries of the world. I am going to examine, whether there be not fome new afpects, in which it may be confidered, if it be true, that, in every hypothefis, it concerns the fafety of the monarchy, and can alter the regular form of the government; whether a friend to the conftitution ought not to perceive, that this queftion poffeffes a factitious importance only, arifing from our decrepit ideas * of the old government; in fine, if it be a matter of indifference, whether a regent be good or bad, and this would very much fimplify the queftion.]*Murmurs.*] And firft, there is a grand afpect,

* Vieilles idées.

under which the question hath been neither viewed nor presented. Not a few philosophers, meditating upon the royalty, have considered hereditary monarchy, as the sacrifice of one family to the liberty of all the rest; every person in the state should be free, that single family excepted. The gulph of anarchy is dug by faction and ambition; Decius leaps into it*; the chasm closes up: and this is the type of royalty according to the theory just mentioned.

"The system of the indivisibility of the privilege, to which all are summoned,

---

* It was *Curtius* rather.—*Mirabeau* quotes from memory, both in profane and sacred story: the facts, and the spirit of them, were forcibly impressed upon his mind, although now and then he confounds personages. W.

and which separates the whole family from the nation, should seem to countenance the opinion, that the nomination of the regent should be vested in the family. The right of the nearest relation takes place, at the death only of the monarch; the question, then, is, to fill up the vacancy; whereas, in the case of a regency, the question is not, to supply the place of the existing king, although an infant, but to fill up the kingly office; and this is a different case from the other. The royalty belongs to the family, the family is to exercise it. Grand words produce no alteration in the nature of things, and the regency, after all, is nothing more than a guardianship.

" Second system. Every king might himself be obliged to name a regent, in his life-time, as soon as he should have a male a male child, or even as soon as the queen should be pregnant. We might, partly, prevent, by that measure, the mischiefs resulting from chance and from an election, and public opinion would incline the monarch to make choice of the most worthy. Our history provides us with several examples of regents appointed by our kings. It was only by testament that kings disposed of the regency; and therein lay the fault; they should have made the disposition in their life-time.

"Third system. Amongst the known modes of election, a multitude of inconveniencies might be prevented, by allowing it to be lawful for the regent elected, to be periodically confirmed in his office, or cashiered; for the making a good choice is the object of the election.

"Is there, then, no mode of election exempt

exempt from inconveniencies? is the subject exhausted? is it perfectly clear, that the true election by the people, is exposed to the same inconveniencies as that made by a handful of aristocrates? And is it drawing a just comparison, to liken, for instance, the elections of Poland, that republic where one hundred thousand gentlemen, all electors and eligible, keep five or six millions of men in slavery, is it just to liken such elections, to those which may be ordered and determined in an empire covered with five-and-twenty millions of freemen, armed for the purpose of making their will respected, by factions internal and external? I might quote a hundred other modes, and likewise canvass the question of a council of regency, appointed as a parallel jurisdiction to that of regent. But all this is not the

the queftion; let us confider it in itfelf, as it ftands connected with the nation, with the king, with the conftitution. To chance are we indebted for kings, and many common-place topics, more or lefs bombaftic, might here be introduced. Let us confine ourfelves to making two obfervations, a little more fubftantial. Chance will often prove fo blind, as to occafion us to lament our inability to correct it by election. I need fuppofe only two mifchiefs, in order to make myfelf underftood; fhould we defire to have for regent, the weak, or guilty, or mifguided man, whom the law might fummon to that ftation?

" This is not all; let us lay our account, for the poffibility of a regency becoming a reign of nineteen years, that is, a reign of no inconfiderable duration;

that,

that, when a king shall be a toothless infant*, the nearest relation shall be, perhaps, an old man, "sans teeth, sans taste, sans eyes, sans every thing †," and that it will be a circumstance truly ridiculous, not to wish to choose a man, in preference to two children. Providence presents us with weak, ignorant, or even wicked kings; but, should we have a wicked regent, we shall have to blame ourselves. So far, as to the nation. And now, gentlemen, for the king, who is the man of the nation, and to whom, accordingly, she owes a double protection. Would you consult the past? our future history will certainly be less tempestuous, than that of our late monarchy, where

---

* Viendra à peine de naître.

† Dans une enfance non moins inactive que celle du roi.

all

all the powers were confounded. Nevertheless, many similar circumstances may yet be reproduced. Now, how many cases are there, in which it would be dangerous, that the nearest kinsman to the crown should be regent? When one does not examine this question very closely, one is at first struck with this idea; since the nearest kinsman might be king, why should he not be regent? But there is a sensible difference between these two cases; a king hath no other connection than with the people, and it is by such connection only that he ought to be judged. A regent, on the contrary, although he be not charged with the wardship of the minor king, is connected with him in a multitude of points, and may, moreover, be his enemy; he may have been the enemy of the father. It
hath

hath been said, that a regent, borne up by popular favour, to which he may have owed his election, might dethrone the king. Take care that this objection hold not with still greater force, against the nearest relation. The former could succeed no otherwise, than by changing the form of government: he might have in opposition to him the sober part of the nation, and all the other members of the royal family. The latter, on the contrary, in order to mount the throne even by virtue of the law, would have but one obscure crime to answer for, and would have nothing then to fear from competitors. Of what signification is it, that the wardship of the king is not entrusted to him? hath he more than one stride to make?

" But here are other objections, drawn from the very nature of our constitution.

Does not the true theory of government conduct us to an elective regency? When a king is a minor, the royalty does not cease; it becomes inactive; it stops, like a watch the spring of which is broken*. The maker of the watch must restore its moving power. The more one searches into the system of election, the more it is found conformable to genuine principles. A regent is but a functionary of the public. Is it the spirit of our new constitution, that every public function should be elective, except the royalty? It is still more the spirit of our constitution, that equality should be respected wheresoever she can exist. Now, an elective regency would preserve a kind of equality †,

---

* Qui a perdu son mouvement.

† In the original, it is the reverse—" inégalité"— Does not the sense bear me out in the alteration I have ventured to make? W.

amongst the members of the royal family.
Again; a regent is, in reality, nothing else than a prime minister unremovable for a certain time; for, during the regency, all is done in the king's name: now, when a minor king is incapable of choosing his own minister, to whom does the choice belong, if not to the legislative body? The order of ideas, then, conducts us to this conclusion, and, consequently, to the system of election. You have already seen what inconveniencies attend the adverse system. Advert now to the national advantages, accompanying the theory of elections. Montesquieu hath well remarked, that, during a certain period of our history, our kings were elective; but, in the royal family, the kingly office had not ceased to be hereditary. Such an election was rather a right of exclusion, than of election. Now,

is it advantageous to the nation, that, in certain cafes, the legiflative body may indirectly exclude, and that it may elect? More talents are requifite in a regent, than in a king. The former naturally infpires us with lefs refpect, and perhaps it is owing to that very circumftance, that almoft every regency hath been tempeftuous*. Now, by election, we fhould

---

* The minifter of a regent is in a much more trying fituation, than the minifter of a king. The fervant of a fervant is generally hated, when entrufted with the exercife of authority.—It is fomewhat fingular, that, in the three laft regencies of France, the chief minifters were none of them natives of the kingdom. Mary of Medicis confided in *Concini*, Anne of Auftria in *Mazarine*, the godlefs Duke of Orleans in Mr. *Law*, the Scotchman. It hath been remarked, however, that female fovereigns are moft apt to make choice of able minifters: " I have chofen my lord treafurer," faid queen Elizabeth, " not for his bad legs, but for his good " head." W.

have the means of provifionally entruft-ing the exercife of the royalty, to fuch members of the fame family as fhould feem moft worthy of the truft: we fhould thus be enabled to give an important lef-fon to the royal minor, by difplaying be-fore him, under the title of regent, the pattern of a good king; but this becomes alfo a ruinous advantage for the nation. If fome reigns of virtuous princes, thinly fcattered through the fpace of ages, have preferved this earth from being undone by the rage of defpotifm, what might not be expected, for the amelioration of hu-mankind, from a few virtuous adminiftra-tions following clofe* upon one another.

" Were it not likewife very ufeful, to demonftrate to that family, placed in fome degree on the outfide of fociety, that its

---

* Rapprochées.

privilege is not so firm, but that the disposal of it may sometimes depend on the will of the nation? That family might even be the better, for adopting such an opinion; for, as each reign could offer to each of them a transitory kingship, they would all endeavour to prepare themselves for it, to render themselves worthy of it; they would all take pains to acquire the good opinion of the public, and to learn the duties of a king. It appears to me, moreover, that an election for a regency would remind us, at certain periods, of the true origin of the royalty. And it is good, that neither the king, nor the people should forget it.

" The elective system, therefore, is very suitable to us, gentlemen, and even very plausible, very favourable, notwithstanding

standing the levity with which, at first view, it hath been treated.

"This question, considered in the elective point of view, hath one great disadvantage, in being discussed for us and amongst us. Sleeping securely* on hereditary royalty, and almost incorporated with it, by custom of the longest date, we have acknowledged it as pre-existent to the constitution, we have not even turned our thoughts to election, because we have no occasion for it. But, assuredly, although it be not necessary for us to solve this problem, it does not follow that the problem cannot be solved.

"What? should we introduce into an institution, which would not involve the avowed inconveniencies attending on

* Assoupis.

elections, the incontestable inconveniencies of heirship?

"But, gentlemen, it is time to present to your observation, the common source of all the errors upon this subject, and especially the extravagant importance ascribed to the different opinions, which have been submitted to your view. We see always, in a king, and in a regent, what those errors were. The former, almost the sole agent of all the good and all the evil, which may befal a great nation, in the course of a long reign; the latter an absolute monarch for several years. But all this is now no more; in a country which can boast of a constitution, in a country where public liberty is built upon good laws, and upon the respect paid to those laws, a king is no more than the supreme executor of such laws, continually
restrained

restrained as well as protected by them, continually watched as well as supported, by the multitude of good citizens who compose the public force. There also a regent, who is only a regent for a certain number of years, is, at bottom, no more than a prime minister, after the most august and most elevated fashion. Undoubtedly, there still exists subject matter for intrigue; there exists, and there ever will exist, a great deal of it, for places, and for employments in the various offices; but there is no food left for faction. When this word is mentioned, upon such an occasion, we think of the Orleanses, of the Condés under Charles VII. of the Montmorencies and the Guises under Francis II. and we forget to think that, in a country where the king is no longer absolute,

absolute, there can no longer be an absolute regent.

"Then falls to the ground every objection against a regent, the child of popular favour, who, soon after assuming the character of an usurper, the succesful rival of all lawful authority, attempts in one moment to subvert the constitution, trample on all the laws, and this amidst the applause and the huzzas of that very nation, whose favour and esteem exalted him to a post, which, like every other, hath its limits, its overseers, its enviers, and its enemies. All this is extravagant, all this is irreconcileable to reason. On the other hand, it appears to me, that, the choice of a regent being in itself a matter of indifference, we had better follow the bent of our inclinations, of our habitudes,

and

and fix the regent beforehand, and in a form that shall not vary; and, to sum up in a few words the advantages which have been shewn to you; 1. To decree, that the delegation of the regency to the nearest relation, is consonant to received ideas; 2. That it were, perhaps, dangerous, to exhibit the spectacle of an elective regency, beside an hereditary royalty; 3. That the relation nearest to the throne is to be supposed better prepared, for performing the functions of the kingly office; 4. That he will be more interested in preventing its degradation, than any other member of the family, inasmuch as he will be nearer to the enjoyment of it. I am, therefore, of opinion, that the plan of the committee may be adopted. [*Murmurs.*]

Upon this first question, the assembly delegated

delegated * the regency, in the direct line, to the nearest male relation of full age, according to the order of the heirship to the throne.

The fourth article of the plan, relative to the conditions necessary in order to become regent, made no mention of taking an oath: it was required that this condition should be added.

M. *Montlaufier* called for a division, as a prince might have reasons for not having taken the oath: he might have been beyond sea—

MIRABEAU.

" I am afraid that the member who spoke last is mistaken; he hath talked of beyond sea; perhaps he meant to say,

---

* Article III. of the decree.

beyond the Rhine." [*This produced a laugh, and the applause of the assembly.*]

The second question was then agitated, namely, whether the election should be made by means of an electoral body, or whether the regent should be appointed by the legislature.

MIRABEAU.

"I do not ask leave to discuss this question, since it is not my turn to speak, and since I have a consideration to offer, which tends to put off the discussion. I think the mode recommended in the plan, unacceptable in every respect. I know not what is meant, by electors assembled for the purpose of appointing other electors, upon an occasion equally unimaginable.

ble. Besides, there are enormous inconveniencies to be apprehended, from transforming, under any pretence whatever, a legiſlature into an electoral body. This appears to me derogatory to every principle.

"In this alternative, it is allowed on all hands, that there is no urgent neceſſity for coming to an immediate determination. We have time enough to look out for a mode, which may accord with the wiſhes of every one. But when the committee itſelf almoſt abandons its own mode of election, when, at leaſt, it feels much diffidence upon that head, perhaps it might be found, that the wifeſt courſe were to adjourn this particular queſtion, and to proceed in our examination of the reſt of the plan."

It was thought that the mode could not
be

be taken into confideration, until they had decreed the principle upon the queftion, whether the legiflative body fhould fay yes or no.

This propofition was admitted, and the affembly decided*, that, in the cafe where it fhould become neceffary to elect a regent, fuch election fhall not be delegated to the legiflature.

The nineteenth article of the committee fixed the time of the king's taking his feat in the council, at the age of fourteen years, without a deliberative voice.

M. *Defmeuniers* propofed leaving out the words, *without a deliberative voice*, and fubftituting, in their place, the words, *for his inftruction.*

* Article VI.

MIRABEAU.

"Let us trouble ourselves no further about the time which shall be fixed, for the royal minor's becoming a member of the council; let us not fix upon the age of fourteen, in preference to fifteen; unless we likewise decree, that nothing shall be agitated there, but stories about Tom Thumb and Jack the Giant-killer*. Let us say merely, that the royal child shall be admitted into the council, as soon as the regent shall think proper." [*Murmurs.*]

M. *Lapoule.* I ask leave to speak, in

---

* Fariboles.—It hath been sufficiently evident, in a former oration, how much *Mirabeau* disliked the idea of admitting raw striplings, as members of assemblies for solemn debate. W.

order to combat the propofition of M. Mirabeau.

MIRABEAU. "Since M. Lapoule is inclined to combat my propofition, I withdraw it." [*More murmurs.*]

M. *Lapoule:* The humility of M. Mirabeau is always attended with fuccefs. Since he withdraws his propofition, I move that the article be worded in this manner:

Article XIX. The king having attained the age of fourteen years complete, fhall be prefent at the council for his inftruction only. [*Applaufe.*]

This amendment was adopted.

The twenty-firft article of the plan propofed, that the king being of full age, fhould announce, by proclamation made through the whole kingdom, that he had attained his majority, and that he had entered upon the exercise of the royal functions.

Mirabeau recommended, that the legislative body being assembled, the king should repair thither, in order to take the oath, and that then the legislative body should cause proclamation to be made.

The assembly adopted the article of the committee, with this addition, "that the proclamation shall contain the king's oath, with a promise to repeat it in presence of the legislative body, as soon as the latter shall be assembled."

April 2, 1791.

DEATH OF MIRABEAU.

We left Mirabeau in the tribune, and already he hath terminated his brilliant career;

career; in the midst of the most astonishing revolution that ever the sun beheld, a premature death hath snatched him from his country, from liberty, from the happiness of mankind. One of the chief founders of the constitution of this kingdom, he was become her chief hope. Eloquent speaker, sublime writer, profound politician! his genius, after having effected the revolution, had forced his enemies to admiration or to silence. Could any other man than Mirabeau, have restored France to that situation, which she had lost under a government both versatile and absurd?— A deep disquietude agitated the citizens, regret and sadness were depicted in every face; his death was considered as a public calamity.

The president, M. Tronchet, desired leave to speak—A mournful presage extorted

torted from his colleagues these afflicting words: *Ah! he is no more.*

He died this morning at half after eight. I will not recal to your memory, said M. Tronchet, the applause which you have so repeatedly bestowed upon his talents; he hath a much nobler title to our grief, and to the tears which we shall shed upon his sepulchre.

[*A melancholy silence reigns throughout the assembly.*]

M. *Barrere*: Mirabeau is dead;—the great services which he hath rendered to his country, and to humankind, are well known; the sorrows of the public are echoed on every side; shall not the National Assembly, also, testify its sorrow, with a solemnity becoming the occasion? It is not on the brink of that grave which is preparing for him, that I call upon you to exhibit the vanity of human pomp*; it belongs to public opinion, it belongs to posterity, to assign him that place of honour which he hath merited; it is for his colleagues to consign their just regret, to the authentic monument of their labours. I move that the assembly, record upon the journals of this disastrous day, a testimony of its grief for the loss of that great man; and that all the members of the assembly, be invited in their country's name, to be present at his obsequies.

This speech was pronounced in a faultering voice. Very many of the deputies mingled their tears with those, which streamed from the eyes of the speaker.

An ecclesiastic from the right, moved,

---

* Vaines distinctions.

that the assembly should order the work of M. Mirabeau upon the successions, to be printed. Yesterday, said M. de Beaumetz, he desired, in the midst of his sufferings, that the bishop of Autun should be brought to him; and, delivering that work to the bishop, he requested, as a final mark of friendship, that he would read it to the assembly. I have no doubt that the bishop of Autun is eager to perform that sacred duty; and I do not imagine that any member will object, to his exercising, in this place, the office of executor to the great man whom we all deplore.

The president gave notice that a motion had been made, for sending a deputation to the funeral of M. Mirabeau. *We will all go, all,* was the animated answer*.

* S'est on écrié.

The assembly then unanimously decreed, that its affliction should be recorded on the journals, that the bishop of Autun [*here the assembly was for some time inattentive and agitated*] should be requested to read the work of M. Mirabeau, and that the said work should be printed.

The plan of the law relative to the successions, was the order of the day. In the midst of the discussion, the bishop of Autun ascended the tribune, with the production of Mirabeau in his hand. A melancholy silence reigned throughout the assembly.

" I went yesterday, said he, to the house of M. Mirabeau, in which I found a great concourse, and which I entered with sensations of sorrow still more keen than those of the public *. That scene of

* With what peculiar grace the French express themselves, on all occasions where the emotions of the heart are concerned ' W.

desolation filled the soul with the image of death: it was every where, except in the breast of him, who was now threatened with the most imminent danger. He enquired for me. I did not suppress the emotions, which several parts of his discourse raised within me. M. Mirabeau, at that instant, was still a public man; and it is also in that point of view, that we may consider his last words as precious fragments, snatched from that immense prey, which death hath just now seized on. Summoning up all his concern for the sequel of the labours of this assembly, he took notice that the law relating to successions, was the order of this day; he testified regret, at his being unable to be present at the discussion*; and on such

---

* " And thou, brave *Cobham*, with thy latest breath,
" Shall feel the ruling passion ev'n in death;
" Such in those moments, as in all the past,
" O save my country, Heav'n, shall be your last."
POPE.

regret seemed to depend the value which he set on death *. But, as his opinion upon the subject now before you, is in writing, he entrusted it to me, that I might read it in his name. I am going to fulfil that duty. Every mark of the applause which this opinion is about to merit, must excite the most lively emotions in the heart. The author of this production is no more; I am presenting you with his last work; and such was the union between his feelings and his thoughts,

---

* This appears to me to be somewhat affectedly, and obscurely worded, in the original.——" Et c'étoit avec des regrets pareils, qu'il paroissoit evaluer la mort "——Does the Bishop mean that *Mirabeau* was sorry to die, as it prevented his attending the debate on the successions? or, that he was glad to die, since he could not attend it?—The sense seems naturally to be this: that the only reason he had

thoughts, both equally devoted to the cause of the public, that, while listening to it, you are almost receiving his last breath."

April 3, 1791.

Deputations and Petitions relative to the Death of Mirabeau.

A deputation from the sections of Paris was introduced at the bar. In consternation at the loss which the nation had just sustained, and desirous of paying the homage of esteem and gratitude to the *manes* of Mirabeau, they signified a wish

had for wishing to live longer, was, that he might have it in his power to serve his country in the National Assembly. W.

that

that he should be interred in the field of the Federation, under the altar of their country.

This beautiful idea was applauded.

New ideas on the fame subject are offered: the department of Paris comes to do homage to the deceased.

M. la Rochefoucault, at the head of a deputation, expressed himself as follows:

" The administration of the department of Paris, hath, for these some days, considered M. Mirabeau as one of its members. It is by this title that, clad in the garb of woe, we are come to speak of him to the representatives of the nation, and to render the tribute of our earnest wish, that the æra of French liberty may become the æra also of homage, offered up to the glory of men who shall have
deserved

deserved the gratitude of their country. We will read to you, if you will permit us, the extract from the deliberation of the directory."

M. Pastoret, procurator-general-syndic, read the resolution of the directory of department. This piece was couched in the following terms;

Extract from the Registers of the Directory of Department.

The procurator-general-syndic said; " Gentlemen, it is scarce a week, since Mirabeau, seated amongst us, presented, with his energetic oratory, the means of regenerating the empire, of regenerating public tranquillity; and already is Mirabeau no more.

" When death vanquished that illustrious American, whose name recalls to our memory

memory all that the moſt tranſcendent genius, the moſt active ſpirit of liberty, the moſt auguſt virtue hath to boaſt of, the French orator, from the tribune of the National Aſſembly, called on France and the whole world to mourn publicly for the loſs. You have juſt rendered to that orator the ſame homage of eſteem and ſorrow; but, gentlemen, by that homage you have not wholly performed your part.

" Amidſt the juſt affliction occaſioned by a death, which, at this moment, may be conſidered as a public calamity, the ſole mean of diverting our thoughts from ſo mournful a recollection, is to ſeek, in the misfortune itſelf, a noble leſſon for poſterity.

" The tears which are ſhed for the loſs of a great man, ought not to be barren

ren tears. Several nations of antiquity deposited in grand monuments, the ashes of their priests and their heroes. The sort of worship which they rendered to piety and to courage, let us now render to the love of human happiness and liberty. Let the temple of religion become the temple of patriotism *. Let the tomb of a great man become the altar of freedom.

"It is well known, that a neighbouring nation religiously reposits, in one of her venerable temples, the remains of those citizens, whose memory public gratitude hath consecrated. And why should not France adopt this sublime example? Why should not the obsequies of her patriots, become an article of national expence?

* Le temple de la patrie.

"But,

" But, with refpect to fuch a wifh, all that we can do, is to exprefs it; it belongs to our reprefentatives, to thofe whom we have fo juftly entrufted, with the care of our laws and of our profperity, to beftow on it an auguft character. Let us haften, then, to make it known to them, and let a folemn decree inform the univerfe, that France at length is dedicating to the defenders of the people, the monuments which, heretofore, were erected to the chance of birth and of battles."

The procurator-general-fyndic being heard, the directory refolves, that a deputation fhall be fent to the National Affembly, to requeft:

1. That it may be decreed, that the new church of Saint Geneviéve be deftined

stined to receive the ashes of great men, from the date of the æra of our liberty.

2. That it shall be lawful for the National Assembly alone, to determine to what persons that honour shall be decreed.

3. That Honoré Riquetti de Mirabeau be deemed worthy of that honour.

4. That with regard to exceptions in favour of certain great men, whose deaths were prior to the revolution, such as Descartes, Voltaire, and Jean Jacques Rousseau, it shall be lawful for the National Assembly alone to make them.

5. That the directory of the department of Paris, be ordered to put, forthwith, the new church of Saint Geneviéve, in a condition fit to answer the end of its new destination, and that the directors be likewise ordered, to inscribe upon the front :

front: *Dedicated to great men, by the gratitude of their country* *.

This addreſs was eagerly applauded, and the anſwer given by the preſident, added to the impreſſion which it had made.

"When the National Aſſembly, ſaid he, heard the eloquent voice of Mirabeau, recommend that public honours ſhould be paid to the memory of Franklin, it little expected that our grief, and that of the whole kingdom, would ſo ſoon aſk for the like homage at the tomb of our late colleague. He was alſo yours, gentlemen, and the National Aſſembly receives with ſenſibility, the wiſh whereby you expreſs the ſenſation of that gratitude, offered up to one of the firſt and greateſt champions of our liberty. You have, gentlemen, at the ſame time, ge-

* Aux grands hommes la patrie reconnoiſſante.

neralized your ideas; and, in the plan which you prefent to us, we perceive with a lively pleafure, that the talents and the characteriftics of the adminiftration, are accompanied with thofe fentiments of efteem and amity, which united you to our common colleague.

" Although the panegyric of that celebrated man, may be found complete in his productions, it cannot be a matter of indifference, to know the opinion which his colleagues had entertained of him."

M. *Fermont.* " I have remarked two diftinct objects in the refolutions of the department; the one, to decree honours to great men, after their death; the other to beftow fuch honours upon one of our colleagues. The firft idea which offers itfelf to the mind, is, to know whether

the

the great man whom we have loſt, is to undergo the examination required by the department. In calculating the effects of human paſſions, perhaps it will be thought, that this ſame examination ought not to be made by the legiſlative body: I therefore move, that the reſolutions of the department be referred to the committee of conſtitution."

The previous queſtion was called for upon the motion juſt mentioned.

M. *Roberſpierre.* " As to the object reſpecting M. Mirabeau, I am of opinion that no perſon can maintain that is not juſt. It is not at the moment, when we hear echoed from every ſide, the lamentations excited by the loſs of that illuſtrious man, who, at junctures the moſt critical, diſplayed ſo high courage againſt deſpotiſm, it is not at ſuch a time, that opposition should be made to motions for decreeing him certain marks of honour. I second with all my might, or rather with all my sensibility, the proposal of the department. As to the other object of the petition, it appears to me to be connected with the cause of liberty and of our country, and I move that it be referred to the committee of constitution."

M. *Barnave.* " The different objects which are before us, are removing from our view, the true point of deliberation laid down by M. Roberspierre. We cannot, at present, pay attention to the mode which shall be adopted, for consecrating the nation's gratitude towards those who have well served her. The details which such a discussion would render it necessary for us to enter upon, would disturb and degrade the deep sentiment with which we are penetrated. This sentiment passes judgment upon Mirabeau, since it is the remembrance of all the services, which Mirabeau hath rendered to the liberty of this country. To pronounce this judgment, is the question at the present moment. I move that a decree be drawn up in the following terms: 'The National Assembly declares, that Honoré Riquetti Mirabeau hath merited the honours, which the nation shall decree to the great men who have well served her.'—Refer the surplus of the petition to the committee of constitution, with an injunction to make their report without delay."

In this manner were both the objects disposed of.

April 4, 1791.

Decree relative to the Honours to be paid to the Memory of great Men, and particularly to that of Mirabeau.

The intentions of the affembly were fully anfwered, by the difpatch with which the petition of the department of Paris, had been debated in the committee. M. Chapelier reported, that the committee of conftitution had been the more expeditious in that affair, as it was evident that the defign was, ftill more to honour the memory of that great man, the lofs of whom the whole nation was at that inftant deploring, than to decree, on the prefent occafion, a public monument to the great men, who had deferved the gratitude of their country. There remains, he further
obferved,

observed, but one difficulty. M. Mirabeau hath desired in his will, to be interred at his country-seat at Argenteuil; but he did not, at that time, foresee the honours which his country was to decree him. It is the opinion of your committee, that the remains of that great man are the property of his country, as he himself was its property, while living. The committee proposes the following plan of decree:

The National Assembly, having heard the report of the committee of constitution, decrees as follows:

" Article I. The new church of Saint Geneviéve shall be destined to receive the ashes of great men, from the date of the æra of French liberty.

" II. The legislative body alone shall determine,

determine, to what persons that honour shall be decreed.

"III. Honoré Riquetti Mirabeau is judged worthy of that honour.

"IV. It shall not be lawful for the legislature, when near the time of its expiration, to decree that honour to any of its members: it shall belong to the ensuing legislature to bestow it,

"V. The exceptions in favour of certain great men, whose deaths were prior to the revolution, shall be made by the legislative body only.

"VI. The directory of the department of Paris shall be enjoined, to prepare immediately the church of Saint Geneviéve, for its new destination.

"On the front of that edifice shall be engraved these words:

AUX

M. DE MIRABEAU.

AUX GRANDS HOMMES,
LA PATRIE RECONNOISSANTE.

" Until the new church of Saint Geneviéve shall be ready, the remains of Riquetti Mirabeau shall be reposited near the body of Descartes, in the vault of the old church of Saint Geneviéve."

The assembly adopted, with transport, the plan of decree presented by the committee.

When business was about half over, the president gave notice, that the funeral of M. Mirabeau would be ready to set out at four o'clock: it was resolved by the assembly, to attend it in a body.

FUNERAL OF MIRABEAU.

Extract from the Monitor, April 5, 1791.

" All the citizens of Paris, all the societies and patriotic clubs, were eager to strew flowers upon the grave of Mirabeau. On Sunday, the society of Friends to the Constitution resolved, 1. to attend his obsequies in a body; 2. to wear mourning for a week; 3. to resume it periodically every year, on the 2d day of April; 4. to cause a marble bust of that celebrated man to be sculptured, on which shall be engraved those memorable words, which he pronounced, the day the king went to the Assembly: *Go tell those who sent you, that we sit here by the will of the people, and that nothing shall expel us but the power of the bayonet* *.

* See Vol. I. of this selection.

" The

" The funeral of Mirabeau took place on Monday the 4th. Never was ceremony more majeſtic. At five o'clock the proceſſion began to form: a detachment of the national cavalry of Paris took the lead; after the cavalry came a body of artillery-men and pioneers, deputed from the 60 battalions; on each ſide marched a deputation of the invalids, compoſed of the moſt infirm. A deputation from the 60 battalions of the national guard of Paris, marched ſixteen deep, preceded by the officers of the état-major, at the head of whom was M. de la Fayette: the hundred Swiſs guards, and the guards of the prévôté de l'hôtel, preceded the muſic of the national guard; the melancholy ſounds which iſſued from the muffled drums, and the heart-rending notes of the funereal inſtruments, inſpired a ſolemn

lemn terror in the soul: the spectators observed an universal and profound silence.

"The clergy preceded the body; the coffin was to have been carried in a hearse; but the battalion of la Grange-Battalière, of which Mirabeau was commander, desired to be the bearers of that glorious burthen: the body, surrounded by national guards, trailing their arms, was borne alternately by sixteen soldier-citizens. The colours of the same battalion floated over the coffin. A civic crown occupied the place of the feudal ensigns*, formerly displayed at the obsequies of particular individuals. Next came the National Assembly, escorted by the battalion of veterans, and by that of soldiers-children. These were followed

---

* His coronet and escutcheons.

by

by the electors, the deputies of the forty-eight sections, the department, the municipality, the judges of the tribunal of Paris, the municipal officers of several neighbouring towns, the society of the Friends to the Constitution, the king's ministers, the society of 1789, and all the brotherhoods and patriotic clubs in Paris. The procession was closed by a considerable detachment of infantry and cavalry. This whole train, which extended more than a league in length, proceeded in the greatest order, between a double line of national guards, and an innumerable crowd of citizens, of both sexes and of all ages. Sadness was visible in every face; many of the by-standers wept, and all experienced that deep and heart-felt sorrow, which a great public loss inspires.

" After moving for three hours in awful

ful silence, the procession arrived at Saint Eustache. The whole church was hung with black. A sarcophagus was erected in the middle of the choir. After the customary service, M. Cerutti delivered a discourse, in which he considered Mirabeau as a politician and as a legislator. In taking notice of his civic virtues, and of the services which he had rendered to his country, the orator drew tears from the eyes of all his auditors. When this discourse was finished, the procession again set forward for Saint Geneviéve. The same order, the same silence was observed. The funeral reached the church at midnight, and the body of Mirabeau was deposited beside that of Descartes. It is to remain there, till the new church, which the National Assembly hath ordered to be finished, be in a state proper for the

the reception of the aſhes of thoſe, whom the nation ſhall deem worthy of that honour *."

* We have now conſigned the illuſtrious French orator to the grave, after having liſtened to him with admiration and aſtoniſhment in the aſſembly. I ſay, liſtened to him; for it ſeemed as if we were preſent, as if we beheld him, as if his voice were vibrating on our ears. Aſſuredly, except the Emperor Peter I. of Ruſſia, this century hath not ſeen a more extraordinary man.

Franklin, Waſhington, Mirabeau—what a glorious triumvirate! I am no republican; I love our limited monarchy in my ſoul; but I cannot forbear contributing my portion of applauſe, to men who have been the aſſertors of liberty.

The excellent and lamented Mirabeau was ſnatched away in the vigour of life, in the zenith of his fame, in the grand career of his philanthropy. He expired at the age of forty-two years. Young man, (for I will not addreſs myſelf to the callous heart of the ſexagenary) young man, who ſhall have happened to peruſe theſe pages, know that what is here tranſlated,

translated, forms but an inconsiderable part of the political works of Mirabeau. I mention this, in order that you may be sensible what wonders can be wrought, by a mind occupied and inflamed with a passion for true glory.

To the praise of the present æra, and as a circumstance of splendour and dignity in the times, be it remarked, and remarked with exultation, that the young have taken the lead in almost every great adventure, which hath promoted the prosperity of mankind. Franklin, indeed, was venerable. But cast your eyes around you; look on England, on Ireland, on Poland, on France,—every thing illustrious, every thing sublime, is there the workmanship of men who are yet in the spring of life. Senates are convinced, abuses overturned, constitutions created, legislation is dignified, the helm of empire guided, laudable and stupendous revolutions are effected, by sages who have yet scarce accomplished their eighth lustrum. They have snatched the sceptre of influence from the jealous grasp of age, and committed it to the hand of virtue; for what is experience, when unaccompanied by integrity? The *Scipios* triumph, and the *Fabiuses* are their detractors.—But these examples are only a few brilliant gems, which sparkle upon the dark foil of dissipation and insignificance.

The funeral honours of Mirabeau, are an affecting and useful passage in the history of the revolution. If you have read with tearless eye, the relation of his death and obsequies, I pronounce that nature never intended you for an orator. Shut up your books upon the art of speaking, abandon your Cicero and your Quinctilian; you may learn to become a tiresome talker, but you will never arrive at fame; for you are destitute of that sensibility, which is the master-key to eloquence.

Abjure the frivolity and corruption of the times, and dedicate your heart to that pure and sterling patriotism, which is the offspring of wisdom co-operating with probity. Become the defender, not the disturber of the constitution. Let public spirit be your counsellor; but, in looking around for models, beware of imitating characters in the gross; discriminate their virtues from their vices; suffer not your understanding to be dazzled and led astray, by those heterogeneous mixtures of worthiness and depravity,

depravity, of ability and infatuation, which are decked by the cunning hand of self-interested ambition, and exhibited as patterns for the young men of the age; nor imagine that there is no mean between the hypocrite and the profligate. Better were it to admire, and select for your archetype, even the regenerated good man, who may erft have been a stranger to the paths of rectitude, than one of those entangled characters, who are, as they ever have been, a tissue of shining qualities and miserable defects, to unravel and sort which, the mind of youth hath, frequently, neither the judgment nor the inclination; characters, in fine, which at once challenge our love, and provoke our aversion.

Have a care also of mistaking a combination of individuals, for the great constitutional party of the state. Mirabeau was of the only party which a wise man wishes to join; the genuine and universal party of the people. Keep your judgment in your own hands: petition God to enlighten your understanding. Disdain (I consider you as an independent man) to wear the trappings of court-favour, or the

livery

livery of a faction. Independence, you will answer, is a vague expression. But be assured, that independence is not to be measured by your estate, but by your mind. Stand aloof from that spirit of luxury and irreligion, which all monarchical governments, notwithstanding devout and well-intended proclamations, ever artfully and secretly encourage. Kings may be solicitous for the purity of their subjects; but there is, in monarchy, a strong and never-resting bias towards depraving the public heart.

The portion of republican blood which flows through the veins of the English constitution, is unquestionably some check upon this malign and destructive principle. The mischief is, with us, less flagrant and less rapid, than it is in despotic governments. But, if monarchy tend insensibly to undermine a nation's worth, the consequences of faction are equally detrimental. The narrowness of conception, the political shortsightedness, the headstrong rapacity, the venomous spirit, the utter contempt and dereliction of candour, the encouragement afforded to every bad passion, the horrid calumnies,

calumnies, and the infernal artifices, which characterize and dishonour both her maxims and her measures, form a grand imposition upon the credulity of nations, and are the scourge and the curse of society. W.

END OF THE SECOND VOLUME.

Lightning Source UK Ltd.
Milton Keynes UK
UKHW020733111218
333785UK00013B/885/P